The Communist Movement in China

THE COMMUNIST MOVEMENT IN CHINA

AN ESSAY WRITTEN IN 1924 BY
CH'EN KUNG-PO

EDITED WITH AN INTRODUCTION BY
C. MARTIN WILBUR

Issued under the auspices of the
EAST ASIAN INSTITUTE,
COLUMBIA UNIVERSITY

OCTAGON BOOKS
A DIVISION OF FARRAR, STRAUS AND GIROUX
New York   1979

Copyright 1960 by Columbia University in the City of New York
East Asian Institute, New York, New York

*Reprinted 1966 by special arrangement with
The Trustees of Columbia University in the City of New York*

Second Octagon Printing 1979

OCTAGON BOOKS
A DIVISION OF FARRAR, STRAUS & GIROUX, INC.
19 Union Square West
New York, N.Y. 10003

LIBRARY OF CONGRESS CATALOG CARD NUMBER: 65-288873
ISBN: 0-374-91464-8

Manufactured by Braun-Brumfield, Inc.
Ann Arbor, Michigan
Printed in the United States of America

Preface to the Octagon Edition

As the Chinese Communist movement grows ever more influential on the world stage, its formative years become increasingly interesting. Historians writing in Communist China tend to present a retrospective image of the Party's history which differs in important details from historical reality. They project the present back upon the past. They could scarcely be expected to do otherwise. Some facts and tendencies are obscured, others magnified and distorted. This selective image does not make their writings valueless. Their work is important and their interpretations must be taken into account. They are reflected in general histories of modern China, often unwittingly. Non-party historians, however, wish to use all available documentary materials and to consider alternative viewpoints in their attempts to understand the well-springs of Communism in China, the infancy of the movement, and the tortuous course through which the Party came to power during nearly three decades of effort.

Five years ago the East Asian Institute of Columbia University published "The Communist Movement in China, an Essay Written in 1924 by Ch'en Kung-po". The work was issued in a small edition for private distribution to scholars and libraries. During these years the significance of the essay, which probably is still the earliest known history of Chinese Communism, has increased. Translations have been made in Japan and Taiwan. The original publication is out of print and in great demand.

There are two principal reasons for the importance of this history. It was written only two and a half years after the founding of the Party by one of its first members, who had, however, withdrawn. At the time of writing, Ch'en Kung-po was non-partisan, and attempted in an academic exercise to give an objective account of the movement. Thus the essay was written long before revisionism had entered the accounts by Chinese and Soviet Russian historians. It escaped the biases which the traumatic events of 1927 and the years thereafter inevitably produced upon all writers, Chinese, Japanese and Western alike. For more than thirty years, Ch'en's essay remained unknown and unread. It could not be doctored to conform to any particular interpretation of the events recorded therein.

The second reason for its importance is that the essay contains four documents emanating from the First and Second Congresses of the Party in 1921 and 1922, which were believed to be lost. Although these precious documents are translations into English, they appear to be accurate and probably complete renditions of the Chinese originals. These four documents are fundamental sources of great historical interest. One or two have recently been reprinted in text books or collections of readings on Chinese Communism. We are happy to offer them to all historians, including those in China. They are part of the treasury of the Party's early history.

In the book which follows, Ch'en Kung-po's essay is reprinted just as he deposited it in the Columbia Library in 1924, except for the correction of a few typing errors and the addition of a few explanatory footnotes. My introduction, written in 1960 after careful study of the circumstances under which Ch'en Kung-po wrote his essay, and which attempts to appraise its historical validity, is reprinted with only minor alterations and typographical corrections. The East Asian Institute of Columbia University hopes that by making these two essays available in a substantial edition, they may contribute to the extension of knowledge concerning modern China.

C. MARTIN WILBUR
Professor of Chinese History
Columbia University

August 1965

CONTENTS

PART I: Introduction *by C. Martin Wilbur* 3
        The Author of the Essay 5
        The Essay 17
        Reflections 44
        Notes 47
        Bibliography 57

PART II: The Communist Movement in China *by*
        Ch'en Kung-po 61

The Communist Movement in China

PART ONE: AN INTRODUCTION

by

C. Martin Wilbur

In January, 1924, only two and a half years after the formal establishment of the Chinese Communist Party, Ch'en Kung- 陳公博, a member of the founding Congress in July 1921, wrote an essay entitled "The Communist Movement in China." This was his Master's thesis at Columbia University. It is possibly the earliest history of the movement in existence. For more than thirty years it remained an unnoticed manuscript in the Columbia Library.

The essay interests us not only because the writer provides some heretofore unknown details of events in which he had recently participated, but also because he reveals the thoughts of a young Chinese nationalist influenced by the doctrines of Marx and Lenin. These ideas may be characteristic of the viewpoint of many young Chinese intellectuals of the early nineteen-twenties, and thus provide an avenue to understanding those times. The essay is particularly important because it contains in the Appendix translations of six documents of the Chinese Communist movement in its earliest years, and four of them are unavailable in any other source so far discovered. The four are:

"The First Program of the Communist Party of China 1921"
"The First Decision as to the Objects of the Communist Party of China 1921"
"The Decisions of the Second Conference of the Communist Party of China 1922"
"The Organization of the Communist Party of China"

The two other documents given in the appendix are known and are genuine documents.

The essay is also important because, having remained unused by historians, it is independent evidence that can test the reliability of other published accounts.

Who was Ch'en Kung-po, and what had been his experience at the time he wrote this essay? I shall set forth what I have been able to learn that provides background for the information in the essay. Thereafter I shall evaluate the information he supplies on the Chinese Communist movement in its earliest years.

Many friends assisted me in this research. Mr. Howard Linton first called Ch'en Kung-po's essay to my attention. Miss Julie How's preliminary evaluation of the essay supported my belief in its importance. Professor Franklin Ho put me in touch with a member of the family who gave me permission to publish the essay and secured answers to several questions. Dr. Tong Te-kong and Dr. Susan Han Marsh provided useful biographical and historical materials, and Dr. Tong read the manuscript critically and offered several useful corrections. Mr. Nathaniel B. Thayer provided some biographical material in Japanese. Mr. Chang Kuo-t'ao secured a copy of *Han Feng Chi* for me and Mr. Robert Burton allowed me to see and quote from the manuscript of Mr. Chang's memoirs. Professor Robert North and Mr. Eugene Wu assisted my research at the Hoover Library at Stanford. Professor John Hazard gave expert opinion on some of the documents. To all these friends go my sincere thanks. Publication was made possible by a grant from the Council on Research in the Social Sciences of Columbia University.

I. THE AUTHOR OF THE ESSAY

A. *A Sketch of Ch'en Kung-po's Early Life*

1. Chen's Youth

The published facts about Ch'en's early life are scanty except for what he provided in his *Han Feng Chi,* 寒風集 , a collection of reminiscent articles and literary works written at different dates, which he published in October, 1944.[1] Biographic sources in Chinese, Japanese, and English are full of contradictions and mistakes. For example, most biographic sources give the date of his birth as the sixteenth year of the Kwanghsu era, or as 1890. However, the correct date was probably the 19th of October, 1892.[2]

His ancestral home was Shang-hang in southern Fukien, but his ancestors moved to Ju-yüan in northwestern Kwangtung. The family was Hakka. Kung-po's grandfather moved to Canton, but the family seat remained Ju-yüan. Kung-po's father, Ch'en Chih-mei, was a military officer, who served as a militia chief in Kwangsi, but resigned or was removed from his post in 1895. He was a leader in the anti-Manchu secret society, San Ho Hui. In 1907 he moved from Canton to Ju-yüan, taking Kung-po with him. There he conspired to revolt, but the rebellion collapsed in 1907 and Chih-mei was arrested and imprisoned, remaining in prison until after the Revolution of October 1911, when he was released. He died in September, 1912.[3]

Kung-po had a happy childhood. He received a classical education but in addition was given traditional military-athletic training and taught to ride a horse. He read Chinese novels as well as history. His schooling was interrupted when he was 15 *sui* to help with his father's secret correspondence, but he managed to get tutoring in English. In 1907 after the discovery of his father's plans for revolt, he was hustled off to Hongkong to escape his father's penalty. There he worked on a revolutionary Chinese newspaper as a proof-reader and occasionally wrote short articles. He returned to Canton in the summer of 1908 but his family was in hard straits: his father in prison, his mother ill, and income practically nil. With the help of a few friends, by keeping pigs, and by taking a piece-work job, Kung-po was able to enroll in a modern school, the Yü Ts'ai Academy where he studied English for three years. He also tutored others in English. It was a very difficult period financially.[4]

After the successful Wuhan revolt of October 1911, Kung-po's father was released from prison, elected as a member of the Provincial Assembly, and appointed a military adviser to the Governor. Kung-po was chosen Chairman of a *hsien* Assembly, and was also a staff officer in a revolutionary army. He was then 20 *sui* and a very cocky young man. Kung-po's father, however, ordered him to give up these offices and enroll in a student battalion. He was in the army only a few months, and very much disliked the experience. After the battalion was disbanded, he taught for two and a half years in his former school and then in 1914 entered the Canton Law College. He supported himself as a reporter. He graduated from the Law College in 1917, but feeling dissatisfied with his education he decided to go to Peking to study philosophy. He departed for Peking in the summer.[5]

2. Study at Peita

Peking National University was an extremely stimulating place for a patriotic Chinese intellectual during the years after Ts'ai Yuan-p'ei became Chancellor in January, 1917, and Ch'en Tu-hsiu became Dean of the Department of Letters. Ts'ai, a revolutionary who combined a classical education with long years of study in Germany and France, brought together a brilliant faculty of independent scholars and intellectual leaders, ranging from conservatives to radicals. Ch'en Tu-hsiu brought with him the popular magazine *Hsin Ch'ing-nien,* (The New Youth), having the French title *La Jeunesse,* a monthly journal of opinion, which became a forum for discussion of intellectual, cultural and social reform. Hu Shih's proposals for literary reform and Ch'en Tu-hsiu's espousal of literary revolution appeared in its pages, along with discussions of the position of women in China, of marriage, of modern education, attacks on Confucianism, advocacy of science and democracy, pragmatism and Marxism, and of the need to create a new, modern Chinese culture. Students in the University were inspired by the critical spirit of some of the faculty members and of *The New Youth.* In January 1919 they founded a student magazine named *Hsin Ch'ao* (The Renaissance). There were many student societies such as an Association of Students to Practice Thrift, a Society for Collecting Folk Ballads, a Journalism Society, a Marxist Study Group.[6]

Kung-po says he was not active in student life; he spent most of his time at his books. His few close friends were mostly from Kwangtung. T'an P'ing-shan was his roommate; T'an's nephew, T'an Chih-t'ang and Ch'ü Sheng-pai, later an anarchist, are among those he mentions in his reminiscences. The two T'ans later were fellow officers with Kung-po in the Kwangtung branch of the Communist Party. Ma Hsü-lun, who was then a teacher at Peita, mentions in his autobiography that Ch'en and T'an P'ing-shan always sat together in his lectures. Mao Tse-tung, in his autobiography, mentions knowing Ch'en as a fellow member of a journalism society. T'an P'ing-shan joined the New Tide Society but Kung-po declined to because, he says, he disliked a person he knew in it.[7]

One of the most exciting events that occurred during Ch'en's student years was the "May 4th Movement," the demonstrations organized by Peking students to oppose the post-war award to Japan of Germany's territorial rights in Shantung. It was an event of utmost psychological and historical importance to the Chinese. The demonstrations began on May 4, 1919, and continued in Peking for more than a month, involving thousands of students, hundreds of whom were arrested. Ch'en devotes several pages of his Master's essay to the demonstrations of May 4th and the subsequent days. "It is very interesting and stirring for me to recall my memories of this period," he wrote five years later. "I was in the midst of the great wave, witnessed the radical movement from beginning to end, the deepening of dissatisfaction among the masses, and the stiffening of resistance. How much in beauty and sorrow this picture resembled the general strike of college students of Russia in the winter of 1898-99!"[8] In his article "I and the Communist Party," written in 1943, he relates that he followed the May 4th procession not as a participant but as a reporter for some Kwangtung papers. He left before the students broke into the homes of two allegedly proJapanese officials; he only learned of the attack later while studying in the library. He says the May 4th movement had little effect upon him.[9]

In his Master's essay, Ch'en follows his account of the May 4th Movement with a descriptive list of some organizations which developed as a result of it and from which future Chinese Communists were drawn. He does not say he was active in any of these organizations, but he identifies himself most clearly with the Renaissance Group. "Now many communists come from that group," says Ch'en, "and the way we think and the results of our thinking have influenced the Communist Party."

3. Early Career

After graduation from Peita in the summer of 1920, Ch'en and his friend T'an P'ing-shan, returned to Canton. They decided to start a newspaper in order to spread the "new culture" to south China, although they had no very clear idea what the "new culture" was. They named the paper *Kwangtung Ch'ün Pao* [Kwangtung Masses]. Kung-po was Editor-in-Chief, P'ing-shan was News Editor and T'an Chih-t'ang was Literary Editor. They had a capital of only 3000 dollars. On the day the first issue was to come out the military authorities in Canton, who were from the neighboring province of Kwangsi, ordered all papers to suspend publication. This was to prevent their giving public support to the Kwangtung general, Ch'en Chiung-ming, who was threatening to take the city. After General Ch'en had taken Canton (October 1920), Kung-po was called upon by his Peking classmade, Ch'ü Sheng-pai, who introduced two protegés of the General, Ch'en Ying-sheng and Ch'en Ch'iu-lin. General Ch'en was offering to place them on the staff of *Ch'ün Pao* and pay a subsidy of $300 per month. The men were accepted to do the detailed work, but Kung-po asserts that he declined the subsidy except as salary for the two men, and insisted the paper would not become the organ of any person. Kung-po and P'ing-shan both held teaching positions and were able to devote only a part of their time to the publication.[10]

B. Ch'en Kung-po and the Chinese Communist Party

1. The Beginnings of Communism in Canton

In 1920 Ch'en Tu-hsiu, the famous radical professor of Peita with whom Kung-po had studied, was turning towards Communism. He had moved to Shanghai and was in touch with Comintern agents. A Communist group was secretly started in May of 1920.[11] Ch'en Tu-hsiu became interested in establishing a Communist Party in Canton. Two Russian agents came to Canton in the guise of merchants and got in touch with the anarchist, Ch'ü Sheng-pai, then with the *Ch'ün Pao* group. Kung-po says they agreed to the Russian's proposal that their group establish a communist party in Kwangtung, starting with a socialist youth corps to publicize socialism in Canton. They agreed because Kwangtung was politically unstable, the Kuomintang was without organization or program, they were distressed at the condition of China, stirred by Lenin's victory in Russia and impressed by Ch'en Tu-hsiu's interest.[12]

They had no difficulty recruiting teachers and students from the colleges in which they taught. An interest in socialism was fashionable even among Kuomintang members. But it was difficult to interest industrial labor. The Party Center advocated that the Youth Corps push into the Mechanics Union, the Seamen's Union and even recruit tradesmen. Late in 1920 Ch'en Tu-hsiu came to Canton on the invitation of General Ch'en Chiung-ming to be Provincial Commissioner of Education. He asked Kung-po to become chief of a publicity office to push forward Communist Party organizational work.[13]

In July of 1921 Ch'en Kung-po went to Shanghai to attend the First Congress of the Chinese Communist Party, taking his bride with him. Many points about this Congress are in dispute including even the date. Since Kung-po's account of the Congress, in his MA essay, will be discussed below, I shall not describe the event here. Kung-po attended four meetings but missed the final one which was held on a houseboat on a lake near Chia-hsing (Kashing). The Conference made a bad impression on him according to the reminiscences written in 1943; his break with the Party about a year later stemmed, he says, from this sour impression.[14]

The facts about Ch'en Kung-po's role in the Canton Party branch in the following year are in dispute. I shall first present his own account in the article "I and the Communist Party."[15] Ch'en Tu-hsiu left Canton for Shanghai after his election as Secretary of the Chinese Communist Party. The most active members of the Canton branch were T'an P'ing-shan, Secretary, T'an Chih-t'ang, in charge of propaganda, and Ch'en Kung-po, who handled matters of organization. Most of the work, says Kung-po, devolved on him. "Strange to say, the Canton Party did not receive a cent of Russian money, had no fixed location, and paid no salaries." The three friends of the *Ch'ün Pao* contributed from their salaries for the expenses of the Party. Aside from Youth Corps members, there were about 20 in the Party itself, about half of them laborers. The principal work was agitating among labor unions. When the Hongkong seamen's strike occurred in January 1922, the Communists were active among the strikers who moved to Canton; they added many seamen to the Party.

Ch'en states he was seriously troubled by the fact that he was responsible for the Kwangtung Communist Party and yet could not respect Communist philosophy, which he regarded as popular propaganda. He could not get adequate materials on Marx and his philosophy nor had Ch'en Tu-hsiu been able to answer many of his questions. He determined, therefore, to go abroad for further study. He decided upon America because of his command of English. Ch'en Tu-hsiu, he says, gave his approval while still in Canton.

2. The Issue of Collaboration with Sun Yat-Sen

After Ch'en Tu-hsiu had left for Shanghai, "a representative of the Communist International named 斯里佛烈 Slevelet," together with Chang Chi, came from Shanghai to Kwangtung. He had been expelled from Java for propagandizing Communism and had now come to China as a representative of the Third International. Kung-po had a talk with "Slevelet" and Chang Chi in a Canton restaurant where Chang (one of the elders of the Kuomintang) raised the question of the amalgamation of the Kuomintang and the Communist Party. This was not the question of the Kuomintang taking in the Communists. Ch'en felt sure the matter had been discussed by the two in advance and they had reached agreement. The interpreter was Chang T'ai-lei, later an important Communist leader. They asked Ch'en's opinion and he disagreed for several reasons. Although "Slevelet" advocated this amalgamation and planned to discuss it with Sun Yat-sen in Kweilin, he left the arguing to Chang Chi. The latter argued that the Kuomintang was old and needed the new blood of the Communists, that the Three Principles of the People and Communism were alike, that the new economic measures which Lenin had introduced in Russia were merely the Principle of the People's Livelihood. Ch'en says that "Slevelet" and Chang went to Kweilin to see Sun but did not see Ch'en on their way back to Shanghai; he heard that little was accomplished by their trip.[16]

3. To Support Sun or Ch'en Chiung-ming

During the spring of 1922 Sun Yat-sen and General Ch'en Chiung-ming were at odds. Sun wished to push his Northern Expedition to unite the country while General Ch'en—theoretically his subordinate—opposed and obstructed the plan. Sun attempted first to break into Hunan from Kwangsi. Unsuccessful, he returned to Kwangtung in April 1922 to deal with General Ch'en and to launch his campaign from Shao-kuan into Kiangsi. General Ch'en withdrew from Canton to his base in Huichow on April 20. Just at this time Ch'en Tu-hsiu, Secretary of the Communist Party, came to Canton to prepare for the first Congress of Socialist Youth to be held the first week in May and to inspect Party affairs. According to Ch'en Kung-po's reminiscent account, Tu-hsiu decided to go to Huichow to see General Ch'en, his former patron, and asked Kung-po to come along. As a travelling companion, Kung-po took his Kuomintang friend, Ch'en Ch'iu-lin, who had been placed on the *Ch'ün Pao* by General Ch'en. Kung-po says he was not in the conference between Ch'en Tu-hsiu and Ch'en Chiung-ming; he spent the day seeing the sights of Huichow with his friend. On the boat trip back, however, Ch'en Tu-hsiu told him the signs all pointed to a military push by General Ch'en and trouble for Canton.[17]

The day before Ch'en Tu-hsiu was to return to Shanghai he had a private talk with Kung-po, who describes the details. Tu-hsiu said that in the impending struggle for Kwangtung the Communists ought to know whom they would support. From the point-of-view of principle they ought to ally with Sun Yat-sen, but from the viewpoint of power they should support General Ch'en. Kung-po does not know whether Tu-hsiu was merely testing him out, but asserts that he, himself, maintained they should unquestionably support Sun, a truly national figure. Ch'en Tu-hsiu replied that they should wait and see.[18] This account has a bearing upon Kung-po's separation from the Communist Party.

In view of the unsettled conditions, Kung-po started preparation to leave for America to study. He lacked money and had to arrange for the care of his mother. Wang Ching-wei gave him a letter of introduction to the Commissioner of Finance, but just then Ch'en Chiung-ming's "revolt" against Sun Yat-sen occurred on June 16. Sun had to flee to a gunboat and Canton was disturbed by many days of bombardment. Finally, Sun left for Shanghai.[19] Because of the revolt, Kung-po's funds for the American trip were held up.

At this time news from Party Headquarters in Shanghai was extremely scarce so T'an P'ing-shan wanted to go there to learn what was up. Kung-po called a meeting which elected P'ing-shan the delegate of the Kwangtung Communist Party to Shanghai. Kung-po, who was busy with his preparations for study abroad, stayed in Canton to look after Party affairs. After the revolt was over, he remembers seeing in the paper that Sun had appointed many delegates to work on the reorganization of the Kuomintang and that Ch'en Tu-hsiu was one of them.[20] Kung-po also reveals how he helped effect the release of Liao Chung-k'ai, who was held prisoner in General Ch'en Chiungming's camp. He reiterates that he did not know General Ch'en but got a confidant of the General to persuade him to release Liao.

4. Party Headquarters Tries to Discipline Ch'en

At this point Ch'en Kung-po had a distasteful experience which brought on his separation from the Communist Party. His preparations to leave for America were nearly complete when suddenly Chang T'ai-lei arrived in Canton bearing a letter from Ch'en Tu-hsiu and instructions from Party Headquarters. Kung-po was requested to go immediately to Shanghai to answer charges that he was assisting General Ch'en Chiung-ming. Kung-po stoutly denied any connection with General Ch'en. He declined to go to Shanghai because he was waiting for his American visa, nor could he waste his precious travel money on such a trip. Chang T'ai-lei then asked why he did not go to Soviet Russia rather than America to study. Kung-po asserts that he felt outraged at Ch'en Tu-hsiu and his old friend T'an P'ing-shan, both in Shanghai, who knew all about his plan to go to America and about his non-involvement with General Ch'en. He gave Chang T'ai-lei a long letter to Ch'en Tu-hsiu asking whether he remembered their recent conversation about the relative merits of Sun and General Ch'en. He added a postscript for T'an P'ing-shan reminding him of their long friendship and collaboration and asking why T'an had not spoken out about the things he knew so well. Next day Kung-po reported the experience to a meeting of the Kwangtung Party and announced that he would no longer perform his Party duties. The Party members were indignant at Shanghai's action. T'an Chih-t'ang and Liu Erh-sung both spoke out, and the entire group advocated that the Kwangtung Party should be independent. Later T'an Chih-t'ang was removed from the Party rolls because he supported Kung-po (he was readmitted two years later), while Liu Erh-sung received a stern warning and some of the others were also punished.[21]

Kung-po makes a strong point throughout the article "I and the Communist Party" that he did not know General Ch'en, was never employed by him nor worked on his behalf. There are writers who assert the opposite. Ch'en T'an-ch'iu, one of the founding members of the Chinese Communist Party, states in his reminiscences published in 1936 that after General Ch'en's uprising against Sun, Ch'en Kung-po helped the General in his struggle against Sun and after repeated warnings was expelled from the Communist Party. Chang Kuo-t'ao, another Chinese Communist Party founder, states in his autobiography that before the revolt Ch'en Tu-hsiu was trying to effect a means of cooperation with the Kuomintang. After General Ch'en's revolt, the Central Committee of the Communist Party in Shanghai wrote to T'an P'ing-shan and other responsible members of the Canton branch ordering them to sever all connections with General Ch'en and declare support for Sun. But Ch'en Kung-po and T'an Chih-t'ang continued to work in the newspaper *Ch'ün Pao* and write articles supporting General Ch'en. After the Second CCP Congress (July 1922), the Central Committee again wrote the Canton branch, threatening Kung-po and Chih-t'ang with expulsion if they did not change their attitude and threatening T'an P'ing-shan, the Secretary of the branch, with severe discipline if he continued to tolerate the defiant attitude of the others. Because the Canton comrades did not fully comply, Chang continues, T'an Chih-t'ang was expelled, Kung-po received a scathing warning and withdrew, and T'an P'ing-shan was reprimanded and temporarily relieved of his duties as Secretary.[22]

These accounts were written long after the fact by people who were not in Canton at the time. Several Japanese sources, late and secondary, link Kung-po to General Ch'en. They say that when the General became Governor of Kwangtung, Kung-po became a secretary in his office, and after his fall from power Kung-po left for the United States to study.[23]

It is worth recalling in connection with General Ch'en Chiung-ming's opposition to Sun Yat-sen some facts in the situation that have become obscured by the later cult of idolatry towards Sun. The General had a record as an anti-Manchu revolutionary in his own right and in 1920 had made possible Sun's return to Canton by freeing the city from control of a Kwangsi military group. He also brought Ch'en Tu-hsiu to Canton as Provincial Educational Commissioner; the leader of the Communist Party was indebted to him. Sun and General Ch'en disagreed on Sun's favorite scheme of a military expedition northward to unite China. Many eminent Kuomintang comrades agreed with the General in his opposition to Sun's attempts. According to Li Chien-nung, "all intellectual circles" urged Sun to resign his presidency, and General Ch'en's action was in accord with the general desire of the people for peace. He mentions Ts'ai Yuan-p'ei as one who wished Sun to give up his plan. The "Brief History of the Chinese Communist Movement," one of the earliest Chinese Communist sources, states frankly that it was evident Sun's northern expedition would fail and that the Communist Party was not sympathetic to Sun though it did not openly support Ch'en Chiung-ming. It says that other groups were also unfavorable to Sun. "The best-educated and the most democratic elements were on Ch'en Chiung-ming's side." It mentions Dr. Hu Shih as one of these. "Many of Sun's friends and followers advised him to give up political life completely in view of his demonstrated inefficiency." As Chang Kuo-t'ao tells the story of the revolt, the advocates of a federation of autonomous provinces, in the southwest, supported General Ch'en and many Kuomintang leaders abandoned Sun. Forty-nine Kuomintang veterans, led by Li Shih-tseng, Ts'ai Yuan-p'ei, Wu Chih-hui and Wang Chung-hui jointly issued a call for Sun to retire. It was a terrible blow to Sun and was probably one of the factors which led him to accept the collaboration of the miniscule Communist Party.[24]

Under these circumstances it would not have been surprising if Ch'en Kung-po had supported the General or if the newspaper *Ch'ün Pao,* with some of its staff in the General's pay, had supported him. But on this matter, which apparently was the issue which precipitated Ch'en's separation from the Communist Party, the limited evidence is simply contradictory.[25]

C. *After Communism*

1. Ch'en Goes to the United States and Studies at Columbia

Early in November 1922, Kung-po sailed for Japan, not even stopping at Shanghai. In Japan Liao Chung-k'ai requested him to return with him to Canton where Liao offered him the presidency of the Law College. Ch'en, however, declined. On another occasion, he saw Liao in Atami. Liao asked Kung-po what he thought about the cooperation between the Nationalists and the Communists. Ch'en told Liao of his earlier discussion of the matter with "Slevelet" and Chang Chi. Liao then proposed they discuss it with Adolph Joffe, which was the first that Kung-po knew of the Russian envoy's presence in Atami. Joffe told him, says Kung-po, that Soviet Russia had ordered the Chinese Communist Party to enter the Kuomintang in order to complete the Chinese National Revolution. Joffe also told Kung-po in great seriousness that China could only fulfill Sun Yat-sen's Three Principles and certainly could not carry out communism. In answer to Kung-po's query, Joffe expressed doubt that Soviet Russia could put communism into effect in Russia even in sixty years! Liao laughed at Kung-po's doubts and said, "When we build a revolutionary party we want one for the present, not one for a hundred years later. We should energetically put into effect the Three Principles of the People and not discuss the matter further."[26]

Kung-po says he sailed for America on February 12, 1923; he registered at Columbia on February 28, paying his fees March 1.[27]

According to the records of the Registrar of Columbia University, Ch'en Kung-po entered the Graduate School in the spring term of 1923 about a month late. He was then thirty years old, though the birth date (28th August, 1891) he mistakenly gave would have made him thirty-one. He took courses during the spring, summer and fall of 1923, almost entirely in economics, and accumulated well over 30 points during his first year of study. He completed his MA thesis, "The Communist Movement in China," and had it approved by Professor Vladimir Simkovitch on January 31, 1924, delivered two copies on February 6 and received the MA degree on February 22. He took courses for two more semesters, the spring and fall of 1924, but he did not achieve the Ph.D degree.

After arriving in New York, he learned from his friend, T'an Chih-t'ang, that the Communist Party in Shanghai had determined that Kung-po must undergo Party investigation because of his disobience of orders to go to Shanghai and to study in Soviet Russia. By then, however, he was already disaffected. However, he decided to make a thorough study of the works of Marx and Engels. He became disillusioned with Marxism but also rejected the economics of Adam Smith and English liberalism, and decided that Sun Yat-sen's principle of People's Livelihood would build up and revive China. So he plunged in to study American "practical economics" in order to benefit China. He reports that he had considerable dealings with the American socialist, Scott Nearing. He supported himself teaching in a Chinese School in New York.

He left America in February 1925 without completing the doctorate because, he avers, he could not afford to pay for printing the dissertation. He jokingly calls himself the "One-Quarter Doctor," since he half earned the Columbia doctorate which was worth half as much as the same degree at Harvard, Princeton or Yale! Kwangtung University where he was to teach paid his travel expenses back to Canton and he returned via Europe.[28]

2. A Sketch of Ch'en Kung-po's Later Career

After his return to China in the spring of 1925, Ch'en had an active career in politics, journalism and government, but none of it bears upon his thesis, "The Communist Movement in China." Therefore I shall merely outline the main facts.

Ch'en joined the Kuomintang as a protegé of Liao Chung-k'ai, and became Director of the Bureau of Workers and Peasants in the Kwangtung provincial government, a position which put him into close working relations and conflict with Communist organizers, particularly in connection with the Hongkong strike. After the assassination of Liao Chung-k'ai in August, 1925, Ch'en became head of the Peasants Department in Central Headquarters of the Kuomintang. He was also for a time acting President of Sun Yat-sen University and chief of the Political Training Department of the Military Council. At the second Kuomintang Congress in January, 1926, he was elected to the Central Executive Committee (CEC), a mark of his political importance. He was by now closely connected with Wang Ching-wei. During the first stage of the Northern Expedition Ch'en was Director of the Bureau of Political Affairs of the General Headquarters of the National Revolutionary Army directly under Chiang Kai-shek. After the capture of Hankow and Hanyang, he was appointed Commissioner of Foreign Relations in the new Hupei provincial government, and also Chairman of the Financial Council of the Hupei government. In Hankow he was active as an agitator against Great Britain. After the capture of Kiangsi he was appointed head of the Political Council of Kiangsi, a position similar to Provisional Governor. In March 1927 he was elected to the nine-man Standing Committee of the Kuomintang Central Executive Committee and head of the Laborers Department of Central Party Headquarters. An important figure in Wuhan governmental affairs on the radical fringe, he supported Wang Ching-wei in the decision of June to break the alliance of the Kuomintang with the Communists.

Thereafter Ch'en's political career was closely related to the fortunes of Wang Ching-wei. He participated during the summer and fall of 1927 in the effort to reconcile the Wuhan and Nanking factions of the Kuomintang, but when results failed to satisfy Wang, both men withdrew. Ch'en supported Wang in his effort to establish a new National Government in Canton, but the Communist uprising of December 11-14, 1927, put both Wang and Ch'en under a cloud for a time. Ch'en was not allowed to attend the Fourth Plenum of the Second CEC of the Kuomintang held in Nanking in February, 1928, although he was a member of the CEC.

As a Cantonese, a leftist, and a follower of Wang Ching-wei, Ch'en was active in the Reorganization Clique in the Kuomintang which opposed the growing power of Chiang Kai-shek. In May, 1928, he started publishing a weekly magazine in Shanghai, *Ko-ming P'ing-lun* (The Revolutionary Critic), which became the widely read organ of the Clique. The journal was ordered suppressed by the Nanking Government in September 1928.[29]

According to a foreign observer, "Students, workers, the younger officers in the army, those who were formerly Communists and are now leaderless, party workers, distressed Government officials who can no longer tolerate confusion—all these classes turn (1928) to Mr. Chen Kung-po for leadership."[30] In December, 1928 he published a book, *Revolutions in Chinese History*.[31] Ch'en also founded Ta-lu University in Shanghai during 1928, but it was ordered closed by the government in May, 1929. On March 12, 1929, Wang Ching-wei, Ch'en Kung-po, Ku Meng-yü and eleven other prominent members of the Kuomintang issued a manifesto denouncing the Third Congress of the Party, to open on March 15, as illegal. The Congress, in turn, "permanently" dismissed Ch'en from the Kuomintang and warned Wang and other members of his leftist group. Ch'en and Ku Meng-yü were editors of *Min-hsin Chou-k'an* (Heart of the People) which advocated continuing the spirit of Sun's 1924 Reorganization, basing the Party upon peasants, workers, and the petty bourgeoisie.

Wang and Ch'en participated in several revolts against the Nanking Government, the most important being led by the northern generals, Feng Yü-hsiang and Yen Hsi-shan, in the summer of 1930. This anti-Chiang movement failed when the forces of the new Government in Peking were attacked by troops of Chang Hsüeh-liang from Manchuria. Wang and Ch'en withdrew to Canton. The Japanese invasion of Manchuria, beginning on September 18, 1931, helped to bring about a partial reconciliation of various factions of the Nationalist Party. A new Central Executive Committee brought Wang and his followers, including Ch'en, back into its membership, and in a governmental reorganization at the beginning of 1932, Wang became Chairman of the Executive Yuan and Ch'en Minister of Industry.

Ch'en served as a minister in the Nanking Government for nearly four years, resigning late in 1935 after someone attempted to assassinate Wang Ching-wei, though he continued as a member of the KMT Central Executive Committee. He published in 1936 an account of his four years in government, *Ssu Nien Ts'ung Cheng Lu*. During 1936 and 1937, he travelled in Europe, particularly in Italy and Germany, returning to China after the Sino-Japanese war broke out. Although he was a member of the Central Executive Committee of the Kuomintang, Chairman of the Committee's People's Training Department, and a member of the Central Political Council, he was not given an important role in government. He was appointed Chairman of the National Government's Committee on Cooperative Enterprises. He was also a sort of "whip" for Kuomintang members in the Peoples Political Council, which held its first session at Hankow in July, 1938.

When Wang Ching-wei left Free China in December, 1938, on the first step of his fateful move towards collaboration with Japan, Ch'en conferred with him in Hanoi. In 1939, Ch'en reputedly tried to dissuade Wang from heading a Japanese-sponsored government, but ultimately followed him into it, becoming President of the Legislative Yuan. In October of 1940, he became Mayor of Shanghai. After Wang's death in Japan on November 10,

1944, Ch'en became President of the Nanking Government. At the end of the war, he went to Japan but was brought back to China for trial, was sentenced to death, and met his fate at Soochow on June 3, 1946.

We now turn to Ch'en Kung-po's MA essay which he completed during January, 1924. That was the month in which the Kuomintang, which Ch'en was later to join, held its First Congress at Canton.

II. THE ESSAY ON THE COMMUNIST MOVEMENT IN CHINA

A. *Some of Ch'en's Ideas*

The essay sets forth the ideas of a young Chinese nationalist of the early 1920's somewhat under the influence of Marxism-Leninism. The economic interpretation of history is central to Ch'en's thinking. The Introduction and Chapter I dwell upon China's depressed economic condition which Ch'en attributes to imperialism. Because of the grip of foreign capitalism, China is unable to solve its economic and social problems. Therefore the people are turning towards Communism, which "sprouts from the soil of foreign capitalism and imperialism."

Ch'en interprets the revolution of 1911-12 as based upon economic causes: the unbearable burden of foreign debt required the overthrow of the Manchus as the first step towards national emancipation from imperialism. However, the revolution was a failure because economic conditions were unchanged. Imperialism encroached even further. The republic failed to solve China's problems and the conservatives attempted to restore a monarchy. This attempt failed. Ch'en informs us: "Where conservatism fails, radicalism will succeed. Where imperialism penetrates, communism begins."

In Chapter II, "The Forerunners of the Chinese Communists," Ch'en draws upon his personal experience as a student in Peking during the period of postwar disillusionment with China's treatment by the victorious Allies. His description of student agitation and action during the May 4th Movement, in protest against the Versailles awards to Japan of German rights in Shantung, vividly recreates the patriotic atmosphere of the time. He tells of the growth of radicalism and the movement to "go among the people" and prepare them for revolution. He then lists and briefly describes six organizations which emerged as a result of the agitations of 1919 and from which the communists were drawn—The Young Socialist Group, the National Labor Union, the Renaissance Group (with which he identifies himself), the Marxian Club, the National Students Association, and the Women's Rights Movement Alliance. Ch'en spots the tendencies in each which led towards Communism. This chapter is an early and valuable recreation of the immediate historical circumstances out of which Communism in China arose.

B. The First Congress of the Chinese Communist Party

Ch'en's essay contains the earliest written account known to me by a participant of the Congress at which the Chinese Communist Party was officially founded. It contains many points of historical interest.

We learn that the Congress, with 12 delegates (whom he does not name), met in Shanghai beginning July 20, 1921, and lasted for two weeks. At the end of the first week, the police interrupted its meeting which then was resumed on a boat in the middle of a famous lake. We learn that the Congress adopted a radical policy of no compromise or cooperation with other parties; set its goals as class war, the overthrow of capitalism, the dictatorship of the proletariat, the ending of private ownership of capital and the means of production; and decided to unite with the Third International. It laid great emphasis on organizing industrial unions, establishing schools for laborers and an institution for training revolutionary leaders. The delegates hotly debated whether Party members could hold governmental office or serve in parliamentary bodies, and whether to oppose Sun Yat-sen and work for the overthrow of the southern Nationalist government. Disagreement on policy towards the Nationalists resulted in withholding the Party's first Manifesto which is therefore unknown. Ch'en also provides translations of two documents related to this Congress: The First Program of the Communist Party of China, and the First Decision as to the objects of the Communist Party of China. If genuine, they are the only known documents from this Congress.

Let us examine the credibility of this information.

1. Date of the Congress

The Chinese Communist Party today celebrates July 1 as the date on which the Communist Party was founded in 1921 at its First Congress.[1] There is much uncertainty, however, as to when the Congress actually was held. Some accounts say May, some give July. Ch'en Kung-po, writing his Essay only two and a half years after the Congress, which he attended, states "The first Chinese Communist Party Conference of national representatives assembled in Shanghai on the 20th of July, 1921."

Other participants have left accounts of the meeting. Ch'en T'an-ch'iu, in his reminiscences of the Congress published in 1936, says that "in the second half of July, 1921," nine guests arrived at a Ladies' School in the French concession in Shanghai. They came to Shanghai to organize the Communist Party of China. The Congress was opened "at the end of July."[2] Tung Pi-wu, in his recollections given to Nym Wales (Mrs. Snow) in the summer of 1937, says "The central Chinese Communist Party had been founded in May 1921, when Ch'en Tu-hsiu arrived in Shanghai for this purpose, together with Li Ta-chao. I was not present at this meeting but joined the First Conference held in Shanghai in July, 1921."[3] Mao Tse-tung, another participant, gave Edgar Snow an account of his life during the summer of 1936, but he does not precisely date the meeting itself. He says,

The Communist Movement in China

"In May of 1921, I went to Shanghai to attend the founding meeting of the Communist Party. In its organization the leading roles were played by Ch'en Tu-hsiu and Li Ta-Chao. . . ." In the next paragraph of Snow's text, Mao says "There was only one other Hunanese at the historic first meeting in Shanghai. Others present were Chang Kuo-t'ao, Pao Hui-sheng and Chou Hu-hai [Chou Fu-hai]. Altogether there were twelve of us."[4] This is all he says about the Congress. Neither Ch'en Tu-hsiu nor Li Ta-chao attended the First Congress, but according to Tung Pi-wu, they had been in Shanghai in May to found the Party; it is possible, therefore, that Mao attended a founding meeting in May as well as the Congress itself.

Chou Fu-hai published his account of the origins of the Chinese Communist Movement in January, 1943.[5] After describing the preliminary discussions which went on during the summer of 1920, and telling a little of his own work as a student in Japan, he says the Shanghai comrades wrote to tell him that they planned to hold a congress of representatives in July. (This was 1921.) Since it was during summer vacation time he could return to Shanghai to attend. Chou names nine other delegates. Other information given by Chou will be discussed below. Finally, Chang Kuo-t'ao has given his version several times. In 1953 he wrote: "I met Mao in May, 1921, when he was invited to attend the first meeting of the Chinese Communist Party in Shanghai. There were twelve of us at the conference."[6] This dates the meeting with Mao, but not necessarily the conference. In his autobiography, prepared with the assistance of Robert Burton in the period 1954-57, Chang states that it was decided to convene the First Congress in Shanghai in mid-June, 1921. As the time drew near, Ch'en Tu-hsiu had not arrived from Canton, but Ch'en Kung-po arrived with a letter from him explaining his inability to get away. Towards the end of June all the expected delegates had arrived. . . . It was decided to open the Congress officially on July first.[7]

Thus, of the six participants whose accounts I have found, taken in the chronological order of their writing, one gives July 20, another the end of July, the third is ambiguous, the fourth gives July, the fifth says it was planned to hold the Congress in July, and the latest gives July 1st, the official date.

There is a similar confusion among histories. "A Brief History of the Chinese Communist Party," an inside account composed probably toward the end of 1926, gives the date as May, 1921.[8] Yu-Ang-Li, writing in the *Communist International* in 1929, says the First Congress took place in June 1921 in Shanghai.[9] Ch'en Shao-yü, writing in 1936 says that "In July-August of this year there took place the Fifteenth Anniversary of the foundation of the Communist Party of China. At its first Congress (in 1921) the Party had only a few dozen members." He also mentions "The first Congress which took place in July, 1921, in Shanghai."[10] One could pile up more evidence of this sort to show that the precise date of this historic meeting is in doubt.

Ch'en Kung-po, who is both the earliest participant to report and the most exact in his date for the opening of the Congress (July 20), tends to confirm himself in the article "I and the Communist Party" appearing in *Han Feng Chi*; this gives much more detail on the First Congress than his essay, but was written nearly twenty years later.[11] He says that "during the first ten days of July" both the Canton Law College and the Normal School where he taught began the summer vacation so he and his bride sailed for Shanghai where they lodged in the Great Eastern Hotel. If his statement about the summer vacation schedules is accurate and if Chang Kuo-t'ao is correct that the Congress convened after Kung-po arrived and delivered Ch'en Tu-hsiu's letter, the first meeting could scarcely have begun in Shanghai on July 1.

At this point we must conclude that the available evidence as to when the First Congress convened is quite contradictory, but Ch'en Kung-po's date of July 20 deserves as much credence as the official one.

Another point has to do with the length of the Congress. There is disagreement as to how many sessions there were and whether they were held on consecutive days. Two meetings stand out in the memory of the participants: one at Li Han-chün's home that was broken up when a spy intruded, followed shortly by the police; and the final meeting on a houseboat on a lake near Chiahsing, or Kashing, in Chekiang.

In the essay Ch'en Kung-po says, "This conference lasted two weeks, and five committees were elected to draft the platform, program, and manifesto."[12] After describing some of the problems discussed, he says, "at the end of the first week of conference, many bills were still under consideration and discussion, when the police agent suddenly appeared ... detectives and policemen surrounded the conference building, but fortunately ten of the deputies warned the others of the danger, and fled.... In order to prevent the repetition of such an interruption the conference was held in a boat in the middle of a famous lake beyond the jurisdiction of the police...."

For comparison, here is what the other participants have said, presented in chronological order of writing. Ch'en T'an-ch'iu says the Congress lasted four days. But he identifies the disrupted meeting as being on the fourth day. After their meeting place was invaded by the police each of the delegates had to search for a night's lodging as it would be unsafe to return to the Ladies' School where they were staying. At the beginning they had counted on finishing the work of the Congress in seven days, but after this incident it was decided to cut the time to five days. However, since they could not find a suitable place to continue the Congress in Shanghai, they decided to meet at Naihu [Nanhu: South Lake] near Tsiasin [Chiahsing: Kashing]. When they arrived there they hired a big boat, bought food and wine, and carried through the work of the Congress. This was the last meeting, and neither Li Han-chün nor Ch'en Kung-po attended since a watch was kept on them after the search had taken place.[13]

Neither Mao Tse-tung nor Tung Pi-wu provides information on this matter. Chou Fu-hai, writing in 1942, says the conferences were held every evening at Li Han-chün's home. When the conference reached the fourth day,

Maring, who was experienced at secret meetings, warned that they must move to a different place on the morrow for their next meeting since they had met at the same place for several nights already and the police must surely have noticed them. The group, however, thought it too difficult to find another place and decided to hold their final meeting at the same locale. The next afternoon Chou was sick and unable to attend the conference. That night he was awakened about midnight by Mao Tse-tung returning stealthily to their room in the Po-wen Girls School. Mao told of the suspicious intruder and of Maring's warning to all to flee. Chou then gives details of the police search of Li's house and the interrogation of Li and Ch'en Kung-po. He says that he and Mao discussed how the conference could be continued the next day, and asserts that he thought of Mrs. Li Ta, wife of one of the members and a native of Chiahsing. It was his idea that they might all meet in Chiahsing to finish the conference. So he went, that very night, to the house occupied by Mr. and Mrs. Li where it was agreed that Mrs. Li should take a train to Chiahsing and rent a boat on South Lake for the meeting. Chou says they notified everybody before dawn and the following morning all arrived at the railway station in small groups. Mrs. Li, who had rented a boat, met them at the depot in Chiahsing. They held their final meeting on the lake amidst rain and fog.[14]

Thus, according to Chou Fu-hai's recollection they met for four days, then the fifth day's meeting was interrupted, but they were able to make plans for the final meeting during the same night and finish the Congress in a different city on the next, or sixth, day.

Next in sequence is Ch'en Kung-po's account in *Han Feng Chi*. He speaks of "the brief session of four or five days," and says that "on all four days we met at Li Han-chün's house." He remembers that they met "day after day" at the same place, a lack of caution which, he says, was a point at issue between himself and the Chairman, Chang Kuo-t'ao. Ch'en did not attend the final houseboat meeting for reasons to be explained below.[15]

Incidentally, Chou Fu-hai says that Maring and Voitinsky attended the meetings and Ch'en Kung-po mentions them as being at the aborted session. Tung Pi-wu also remembers two delegates from the Comintern who attended this conference; one from Holland whom they called Malin, and the other a Russian whose name he had forgotten.[16]

Chang Kuo-t'ao is particularly at odds with Ch'en Kung-po's account in *Han Feng Chi,* which he had read. He speaks of a few days of discussion but does not say how many meetings there were. However, July 1 is the date he gives for the start and he dates the aborted meeting as July 8. He asserts that this was the only meeting held at Li Han-chün's house and also that neither Maring nor Voitinsky attended any of the meetings of the Congress. Maring was purposely left out, he says, because he was disliked by Li Ta and Li Han-chün, but was invited to an evening meeting on July 8 because he wished to speak on the constitution. Before the meeting was called to order a suspicious person appeared and the group dispersed—except for Li Han-chün and Ch'en Kung-po—before the arrival of the French police. The next morning, says Chang, he contacted Ch'en Kung-po because it was unsafe to contact Li Han-chün. The wife of Li Ta had suggested they meet in her home village on the shores of South Lake in Kashing where she could get a boat. On July 10 they all boarded the morning train separately and after arriving at Kashing, boarded the houseboat and held their meeting. It was attended by all except Ch'en Kung-po, who begged off because his wife was still suffering from her fear aroused by the incident of the night before[17]—that is, the police interrogation of her husband.

Hsiao Shu-tung, who did not attend the Congress, has a curious account. He claims that, as Mao Tse-tung's close friend, he came to Shanghai at the time of the Congress and went to the address on Valon Street in the French Concession where Mao was staying. Mao was not there but returned in the evening and told Hsiao of the trouble with the secret police, who held them for lengthy interrogations. The delegates scattered widely, kept in contact indirectly, and had to remain inactive for several days. Hsiao asserts that one day Mao told him of their new plan to go to Chiahsing, pretending to be tourists going to Hangchow. Mao invited Hsiao to go with him and after the meeting to visit Hangchow. Next morning they boarded the train and got off at Chiahsing. The other delegates gave no outward sign of recognition as they walked away from the station. He and Mao took a room at an inn and Mao went off to the meeting. He returned late at night, and Hsiao discussed Communism with him till nearly dawn.[18]

If this is a factual account of Hsiao's personal experiences, it indicates that several days elapsed between the raided meeting and the final one on the houseboat.

From this array of reminiscent accounts it seems the group met five times, but the fourth meeting was disrupted and business was completed at a fifth session on the lake. The minimum elapsed time would be five days, allowing no days to be lost between the fourth and fifth sessions. There is considerable evidence to refute Chou Fu-hai's recollection that no time was lost in arranging the houseboat meeting; it probably took at least one day between, as Chang Kuo-t'ao recalls it. But Chang has an elapsed time of ten days, while Ch'en Kung-po states in his MA essay that the conference lasted two weeks. The invaded meeting, according to him, came at the end of the first week of conference, which is very close to Chang Kuo-t'ao's July 8, or the eighth day of the Congress. Since Ch'en did not attend the final meeting he may not have known how soon it was held after the meeting at which the police caught and interrogated him.

I have been unable to find a contemporary newspaper report of the police raid which would fix its date. There is, however, an interesting clue.

In *Han Feng Chi,* Ch'en tells about the police raid, and then gives a vivid account of an event that occurred in the middle of the night after he returned to the Great Eastern Hotel. The night was unbearably hot and he and his wife had difficulty getting to sleep. Then, partly awakened by a violent rainstorm, Ch'en thought he heard a shot and a moan. He jumped up and flung open the door but heard nothing more and went back to sleep after telling his wife about his "dream." At about nine o'clock a servant rushed in with the news that a woman had been murdered in the next room. The servant said that the day before a man and woman had entered the hotel, and on this morning the man had arisen, ordered a bowl of noodles, and then started to leave the hotel. Asked for payment, he had said his wife was still in the room and he expected to return. Later the servant had gone into the room to sweep up and found a woman dead upon the bed. The manager came immediately and found a bullet in her body and a towel tied about her neck. Apparently the man had shot her once but failed to kill her and so had used the towel to strangle her.

Ch'en says he feared he might be questioned by the police about the case and thus be discovered as one of those questioned after the raided meeting. Therefore, he and his wife promptly decided to take a trip to Hangchow. There he read in a newspaper some details of the case. The couple, being unable to marry, had decided to die together. As fate would have it, the man's shot did not kill the girl and so he used the towel to kill her. Probably having a sudden change of heart about killing himself, the man wrote a long letter of confession and left.[19]

These details can be confirmed by an account of the case in the *North China Herald* of August 6, 1921, thus fixing the date for the fourth meeting which was interrupted by the police raid. Under the heading "Singular Tragedy in Chinese Hotel," the account tells of a young man with a criminal record who had gone to the Great Eastern Hotel "last Friday"—[that is July 29]—with a young woman and registered as a merchant. About noon on Sunday—[that is July 31]—he was walking out of the Hotel and was asked to pay his bill. He said his wife was still in the room and he would return. About 7 pm a servant went to the couple's room and found the woman dead on the floor. She was wounded in the left arm and thigh, apparently by a single shot, and a towel had been tied around her neck. On the floor was a 32-calibre pistol and on the table were five letters written by the man stating that he and the woman had planned to die together. Several mis-fire cartridges on the floor may show the man did try to kill himself. There was also a letter to a Chinese newspaper asking full publicity for the case.[20]

The details which Ch'en remembered in 1943 of that incident in 1921 are so close to the facts reported in the *North China Herald*, that they appear to date the aborted Communist meeting as Saturday evening, July 30. There are some discrepancies—Ch'en implies the discovery of the dead woman was made in the morning while the *Herald* gives it as evening.

Perhaps we should not exclude the possibility that Ch'en's memory played tricks twenty-two years after the event, and led him to coalesce the police search of the fourth meeting and what he heard and read about a murder in the hotel where he had been staying. If the murder did not happen on the same night as the police raid, it at least provides a terminal date:

the disrupted meeting probably occurred within a few days of July 30. If this deduction is correct then the two dates—July 20 which Ch'en gave in 1924 for the start of the Congress, and July 30, the date of the murder which he recalled in 1943—may approximate the period of the First Congress.

2. Reliability of Information on the Congress

How reliable is Ch'en's information about the work of the Congress, about its debates and decisions? Given the academic nature of his Essay, written after a year's absence from China; in view of the early date at which he wrote, before official interpretations had been fixed and before the bitter controversies within the Communist Party and between it and the Kuomintang had developed as a consequence of the 1927 split; and considering the independent position he was in—at least psychologically out of the Communist Party but not yet in the Kuomintang—given these conditions there is some presumption of objectivity in his reporting.

Ch'en gives three types of information—simple factual detail, reports on matters debated, and documentary data. These may be evaluated separately.

Some of the simple factual detail can be easily corroborated from other, independent sources. An example is the statement that there were 12 delegates representing seven sections—Canton, Peking, Hunan, Shanghai, Shantung, Tientsin, Hankow and Chinese comrades in Japan. Ch'en T'an-ch'iu, Tung Pi-wu and Chang Kuo-t'ao list the same 13 delegates (with variations in romanization), and Chang explains that one of them, Ho Shu-heng, was sent back to Hunan by Mao Tse-tung on a pretext to get him away from the conference, so that there were actually 12. All three lists locate the delegates as coming from the same centers as Ch'en Kung-po does, except that none mentions Tientsin. Apparently Ch'en slipped in listing Tientsin.

Another factual detail, the date and length of the Congress, has already been discussed. The accounts of the police raid and the final meeting on the lake, are confirmed by Ch'en T'an-ch'iu, Chang Kuo-t'ao, Chou Fu-hai, and Hsiao Shu-tung while the police raid is mentioned in "A Brief History of the Chinese Communist Party." Though Ch'en did not attend the final meeting, his one-sentence description shows a close knowledge of it. In factual detail Ch'en scores well.

Yet he left out some details which he knew: the names of the delegates, the fact of his own participation, and the presence of Comintern advisers at least in the background.[21]

Ch'en gives us no feel for the range of opinion which apparently prevailed at the Congress, to judge by the "Brief History" and the reminiscent accounts of Ch'en T'an-ch'iu and Chang Kuo-t'ao, who particularly identify Li Han-chün and Kung-po himself as being rather academic Marxists and part of "a sitting on the fence" group.[22]

On more complex matters such as issues debated at the Congress we should expect differing reports from various sources. In reporting, each participant may be influenced by his own views on the merits of the issue. Furthermore, once an official "line" has been fixed, later reporters—if they are good Party members—will probably be influenced by that line.

Ch'en mentions two issues which caused serious debate. One was the article in the Party's program which forbade members to be officials or members of assemblies or even principals of schools or presidents of colleges if appointed by the government. Opponents held that educational work should not be classed as official service, and that members of the Party ought to be active wherever possible, even in government positions. Because those who opposed the regulation could not be won over, decision was reserved for the next conference. Ch'en's attitude here is neutral; he simply reports. Tung Pi-wu recalled sixteen years later that "one of the points of debate was whether or not officials and technical workers could be members of the Party. Some opposed this. The resolution passed was for a 'closed door' policy, to keep the membership secret and 'pure'."[23]

The second issue mentioned by Ch'en was whether in the Manifesto of the Congress, the southern government of Sun Yat-sen should be denounced and attacked equally with the northern government. A minority argued that the platform of the Nationalists, in spite of many wrong points of view, more or less represented the new tendency, and that Sun's principle of general welfare resembled state socialism. The majority insisted that because the Nationalists opposed the Communists, the southern government should be overthrown. (Ch'en does not state whether he was with the majority or minority.) Finally the manifesto was passed, but the next day it was decided to leave to the Central Executive Committee the question of its publication. It was not issued and "that manifesto is now not known to the world."[24] Tung Pi-wu tends vaguely to confirm this: "We decided upon an anti-imperialist, anti-militarist manifesto, but we haven't a single copy of this first document of the party."[25] Ch'en T'an-ch'iu confirms a debate over Sun Yat-sen, which he places on the last day of the conference (in which Kung-po did not participate). He says Pao Hui-sheng (a delegate from Canton) opposed Sun and advocated treating him the same as the northern militarists. This conception, says Ch'en T'an-ch'iu, was rejected by the delegates who adopted the following line: "In general a critical attitude must be adopted towards the teachings of Sun Yat-sen, but his various practical and progressive actions should be supported by adopting forms of non-Party collaboration. The adoption of this principle laid the basis for further collaboration between the Communist Party and the Kuomintang. . . ."[26] Thus he confirms the debate over policy towards Sun but contradicts Ch'en Kung-po as to the decision. This difference can be explained by the fact that Kung-po did not attend the final meeting; but Ch'en T'an-ch'iu's 1936 account may also be explained by the fact that collaboration with Sun Yat-sen later became the keystone of CCP policy—in short, he may have been reading later official policy back into 1921.

Kung-po elaborates in his 1943 article. He says he strongly objected to the passing of the Manifesto which equally criticized Sun and Hsü Shih-ch'ang, the rival Presidents of south and north. After the Manifesto had been passed he searched out Chou Fu-hai and Li Han-chün and discussed methods to repair the situation. Finally in the last session (he must mean the third) he proposed an amendment—that the question of publishing the Manifesto should be left to the decision of the newly elected Secretary. After returning to Canton, Ch'en argued the matter with Ch'en Tu-hsiu, the new Secretary, who decided not to issue the Manifesto. That is why, says Ch'en, there is no Manifesto among the documents of the First Congress of the CCP.[27]

To conclude—the 1924 essay identifies two important debates that were later also remembered by others. Ch'en's reports of the outcome seem at least as credible as later accounts. His presentation seems objective and he withheld his own views even though he had been strongly involved as we learn from his later writing.

3. Authenticity of the Documents

Much of Ch'en's account of the decisions of the First Congress is drawn directly from the two documents he gives in Appendix 1 and 2. According to the Essay's Table of Contents each of the six appendices is translated from Chinese.

I have been unable to find a Chinese text of these two documents nor any other version of them. Are they authentic? If they are unique, their authenticity can only be inferred from the preponderance of evidence.

Two of the six documents (Appendix 3 and 6) are available in Chinese.[28] From these we can see that Ch'en did have some documents available in New York when he wrote the Essay. His translation of the two extant documents is generally faithful, though many of the English terms he used do not accord with the present customary Communist nomenclature.

We know that the First Congress did have documents before it. The "Brief History" says Ch'en Tu-hsiu sent his draft of a Party platform to be discussed at the meeting. Ch'en T'an-ch'iu mentions that just before the police descended on the meeting in Li Han-chün's apartment "we quickly gathered together our documents and disappeared." He also mentions the final endorsement of the Party statutes. Chang Kuo-t'ao, after describing the decisions taken at the final houseboat meeting, says the newly elected Central Committee was to take the various resolutions of the Congress and turn them into Party documents. Chou Fu-hai says the constitution and regulations on organization were adopted at the houseboat meeting. Tung Pi-wu says that "all the historical data of this first conference have been lost."[29]

Considering the disruption of the fourth meeting, which was not actually held, and the speed-up required at the fifth meeting on the houseboat, it seems likely that final texts of decisions or resolutions had to be produced by a post-conference committee. In any case, Kung-po probably did not take any documents with him from Shanghai. This is deduced from his own later reminiscences. He tells that when the fourth meeting in Li Han-chün's house was raided the others all fled, but he remained with Li. Three French police and four Chinese plainclothesmen thoroughly searched the rooms. They saw but did not recognize the significance of a piece of paper on which was scribbled an outline of the organization of the Communist Party. The police did notice a number of books and articles on socialism but were apparently satisfied with Han-chün's explanation that he was an editor for the Commercial Press and therefore read all sorts of books. Both men were interrogated at length. After the police left, Kung-po started back to his hotel but saw he was being followed. He lost his pursuer in the movies of the Great World amusement place, hurried back to the hotel where he locked his door and burned his papers. He did not attend the final meeting on the lake.[30]

It is quite probable that, if documents were produced representing the decisions of the Congress, Kung-po would have them. During the subsequent year he was one of the leaders of the Canton Party branch, in charge of organizational work. He was still a Party member when he left for the United States in November, 1922, though alienated. Whether he took some documents with him or, more likely, wrote back to Canton for materials when he had decided on his Master's topic, we can only speculate.

It is interesting that the captions for Appendices 1 and 2 do not ascribe them to the First Party Congress. One is called "The First Program" and the other "The First Decision as to the Objects of" the Communist Party of China 1921. In contrast, Appendix 3 is captioned "The Manifesto of the Communist Party of China Adopted in July 1922 by the Second Congress." Appendix 4 is captioned "Decisions of the Second Conference . . ." Nevertheless, Ch'en uses the first two appendices as documents of the Congress and builds his description of decisions on them.

A few of the specific points Ch'en draws from these documents are supported by other participants or early sources, but one is disputed. Ch'en T'an-ch'iu supports Kung-po that one of the important decisions was to adopt the dictatorship of the proletariat, and that the chief aim of the party is to form industrial unions. He says, "At last the general line was accepted, in which the main task of the Party was recognized to be the struggle for the dictatorship of the Proletariat. . . . The development of the trade union movement was put forward as a central task of the work of the Communist Party."[31]

A point in dispute is whether the Congress decided that the Chinese Party should join the Third International (that is, the Comintern). Ch'en says the delegates did so decide. Besides drawing upon his memory, Kung-po had before him Appendix 1, The First Program, which says, "2. The programs of our Party are as follows: . . . D. To unite with the Third International." His Appendix 2, The first Decision as to the Objects . . . of the Party says,

> " (6) The relation between the party and the Third International. The Central Organ should make a report to the Third International each month. If necessary, a formal representative should be sent to the station in the Far East Secretariat of the Third International in Irkuchika and deputies should be sent to the various Far East nations to further plans for union in the class struggle."

Ch'en T'an-ch'iu contradicts Kung-po on this decision. He says that during the First Congress the Party had no organizational link with the Comintern. It was officially decided at the Second Congress to join the Comintern.[32] The "Brief History," after describing the mildness of Ch'en Tu-hsiu's draft program and the unfavorable attitude of Li Han-chün towards the Russian Communist Party, says "It is obvious that with such opportunistic currents of thought at the Congress, it was impossible to discuss or even raise the question of the Chinese Communist Party joining the Comintern."[33]

These two sources, one written in 1936, the other in 1926, certainly contradict Ch'en Kung-po. Which is right?

In that admirable documentary survey *Soviet Russia and the East, 1920-1927* by Xenia Joukoff Eudin and Robert C. North, we learn that in 1920 a Special Department of the Far Eastern Secretariat of the Comintern was established in Irkutsk, which began publication of a weekly bulletin in February, 1921, and this gave way to a regular journal published in Russian and English beginning probably in May 1921. Its chief editor was B. Z. Shumiatsky. In the spring of 1920 the Far Eastern Secretariat of the Comintern sent two agents to China, one of whom was Grigorii Voitinsky, the same who later probably attended the First Congress of the Chinese Communist Party. In the spring of 1921, before the Congress, Chang T'ai-lei, who had attended a conference in Shanghai the previous September to discuss the formation of a Communist Party, arrived in Irkutsk to establish closer contact with the Far Eastern Secretariat, which instructed him to prepare a report to deliver at the Third Congress of the Comintern soon to be held in Moscow. Another Chinese Communist, Yang Ho-te, also had come to Irkutsk, and the two held conferences with representatives of the Far Eastern Secretariat, as a result of which a Chinese Section of the Far Eastern Secretariat of the Comintern was established.[34]

The author of this information is none other than Shumiatsky who was in Irkutsk at the time. The information is in a memorial article he wrote in 1928 for Chang T'ai-lei, who had lost his life in the Canton Commune in December 1927. According to Shumiatsky, Chang T'ai-lei, at one of these sessions of the Chinese Section in the spring of 1921, outlined the duties of the section as follows:

> 1) A Chinese Section of the Far Eastern Secretariat (in Irkutsk) is established to attend to the problems connected with the relations between the Chinese Communist Party and the Comintern, to supply information to the Chinese Communist Party and to the R.S.F.S.R., as well as to pass on the directives of the Executive Committee of the Comintern to the Chinese Communist Party.
>
> 2) Two secretaries are in charge of the Section: one is delegated to this work by the Central Committee of the Chinese Communist Party, and the other by the Far Eastern Secretariat.
>
> 3) The Section follows the pattern of Comintern organization by which

the Communist parties of separate countries serve as Sections of the Comintern. Likewise, the relations between the Central Committee of the Chinese Communist Party and the Far Eastern Secretariat of the Comintern must be based on the similar principle of organizational contact, that is, the membership of the Chinese Section of the Far Eastern Secretariat will consist of the local representative of the Central Committee of the Chinese Communist Party in the Far Eastern Secretariat, and the Section itself will be subordinated to this Secretariat.[35]

Chang and Yang left Irkutsk in June 1921 to attend the Third Congress of the Comintern in Moscow.

I do not know on what document Shumiatsky based his quotation from Chang T'ai-lei. He was probably anachronistic in referring to a Central Committee of the Chinese Communist Party or even of the Party itself, since the first Congress had not yet been held, although there were already several Communist-minded leaders and groups in China with whom Voitinsky had worked. Yet Chang T'ai-lei in Irkutsk in the spring of 1921 could have expected a Central Committee to be formed.

In any event, Ch'en Kung-po's document which speaks of the Central Organ reporting to the Third International and the possibility of sending a formal representative to the Far East Secretariat of the Third International in Irkuchika, seems very much in tune with the events of mid-1921; much more so than those later writers who deny any connection with the Comintern.

4. The Two Earliest Documents

Until now, no documents resulting from this First Congress have been known to be preserved; Tung Pi-wu thought all of them had been lost. Appendix 1 and 2 may be, and I believe are, documents embodying the decisions of the First Congress.

Appendix 1

"The first program of the Communist Party of China 1921" is a charter of organization stating name, purpose, and rules for membership, and party structure. The pattern of organization is very simple. A year later, as evidenced by Appendix 5, the rules of organization would be considerably more detailed.

The objectives of the Party, here called "programs," are stated to be: overthrow of the capitalist class by the proletariat and elimination of classes; dictatorship of the proletariat until classes have been abolished; and overthrow of private ownership of capital and institution of social ownership. Rules for membership are elementary: anyone who accepts the programs and policies of the party, promises loyalty, cuts off relations with other parties, and is introduced by a member may become a comrade after a two-month period of investigation and election by a majority of the members.

The system of organization centers about the local "soviet," which would probably have been better translated "cell." While clearly derivative from Communist Party organization elsewhere, the system is here quite simple. A local "soviet" of less than ten members has only a secretary; one with more than ten should have a treasurer, organizer, and propagandist; one with more than thirty members should have an executive committee, the rules for which would be stipulated later. No hierarchy of organization is described at local, intermediate and national levels, but it is anticipated that a Central Executive Committee will be elected by a National Representative Conference when there are over 500 members. Until then a Provisional CEC should be organized. Members of the Party are normally forbidden to be government officials or members of parliament.

While secrecy is enjoined on members in article 6, we get no sense of a centralized and tightly disciplined party as later was the case. This naiveté seems appropriate to this elementary stage of the Chinese party's development.

In Ch'en's translation there is no eleventh article. Whether he skipped an article or misnumbered the articles thereafter is impossible to tell. The parenthetical footnote to article 14 seems clearly added by Ch'en himself.

Professor John N. Hazard of Columbia University, an expert on Soviet law and Communist system of government, kindly examined three of the appendices and commented on them. Of this first program he said: "The contemporary program in Russia was adopted March 18-23, 1919 by the 8th Congress of the Russian CP. This program in Russia was adopted *after* the victory of the revolution, so perhaps the comparable program is that of 1903, adopted at the II Congress of the Russian Social Democratic Party.

"The Chinese program is really a combined Program and Charter of Organization. Its program is very brief, bearing no comparison to the long review of Marxist theory in the Russian program of 1903.

"The pattern of organization is very simple with no hierarchy of organizations, the local 'soviet' being the major subject of the rules. This Russian word 'soviet' is never used for the local level of the CP and I am surprised to see it here. The Russians call the local level a 'cell' or 'yacheika.' In 1903 the Russian Party had a Soviet, but it was a single top executive council which was at the top of the CP hierarchy.

"The Russian Party's rules or charter as adopted in 1903 are complicated and evidence sophistication in draftsmanship. The Chinese rules bear no comparison."

If we compare Ch'en's Appendix 1 with the Program of the Communist Party of the Soviet Union, adopted at the 8th Congress of the Party, March 18-23, 1919 we find no relation between the simple Chinese program and the elaborate spelling out of theory and plans by the Russian Party.[36]

Appendix 2

"The first Decision as to the objects of the Communist Party of China 1921" seems an important document for the early history of the Chinese party for it lays out a program of action. It gives a glimpse of what the Chinese leaders considered important and how they planned to proceed. There are six topics. They planned to organize industrial unions; conduct propaganda through publishing magazines and pamphlets; establish training schools for laborers; and to create an institute for training party workers and for research. General principles are laid down for each of these enterprises which are quite interesting, if somewhat vague.

Of the two remaining topics, the Decision declares a position of political independence: ". . . our party should stand up in behalf of the proletariat, and should allow no relationship with other parties or groups"; it also plans for relations with the Communist International and anticipates sending representatives to other Far Eastern nations to plan for "union in the class struggle."

The "Brief History of the Chinese Communist Party," written probably late in 1926, confirms that the first four of these plans were indeed carried out during the Party's first year. Chinese Communists worked very hard to organize industrial labor unions, particularly in Shanghai, Peking and Tientsin. The Party established a publishing office to issue translations of Communist classics. Though the enterprise was not very successful, magazines had already been published. The "Brief History" describes one evening class for railway workers at Chang-hsin-tien near Peking which was helpful to the Party in gaining leadership among them. The "Foreign Language School," which had already been organized in Shanghai, was a center of Communist propaganda and systematic training of Party members.[37] The matter of relations with other parties, particularly Sun Yat-sen's Kuomintang, and with the Comintern has been discussed above.

Commenting on this document, Professor Hazard said: "I know nothing comparable in the Russian CP, although the substance of the document conforms to what the Russians had done to labor unions and periodicals. There may have been some such instruction on relations with other political parties after the revolution, but I have not seen it."

This appendix contains one sentence in parentheses which may have been supplied by Ch'en.

C. *The Second Congress of the Chinese Communist Party*

There is some uncertainty about when and where this Congress was held, and who attended. Few if any reminiscences by participants provide details. The present official Chinese Communist version seems to be that the Congress met in Shanghai in July, 1922, with 12 delegates representing 123 members.[38] The "Brief History" dates it June and July, 1922, and says more than 20 delegates attended but does not say where it was held. It mentions that on July 12, 1922, "at the close of the Second Congress," Ch'en Chiung-ming staged a political coup in Canton and drove out Sun Yat-sen. The "Brief History" is in error on the date of Ch'en's coup, which was June 16.[39] Pavel Mif, writing in 1937, says it was held in July with 20 delegates. Hua Kang in his two-volume history of the Chinese liberation movement published in 1940 says it was held in Hangchow in July with 20 delegates of about 100 Party members. Brandt, Schwartz and Fairbank in their *Documentary History of Chinese Communism* say it was convened at Canton, May-July, 1922, apparently basing themselves on Japanese sources.[40] In his reminiscences, Chang Kuo-t'ao says that the Congress convened about July 10, 1922, in Shanghai with nine official delegates and some observers of whom he names two. After hearing a series of reports the Congress was suspended for about a week while a Manifesto was drafted, then met again to ratify the Manifesto and elect a new Central Committee.[41]

Ch'en Kung-po did not attend the Second Congress. He was in Canton active in newspaper work but was still within the Communist movement and remained in it for some months thereafter. His account, together with his three documents, is the most extensive treatment of the Second Congress I have seen.

Ch'en says the Congress was held in Shanghai and that more than 18 provinces sent representatives. Appendix 5—a sort of Party regulations or statutes —says in the last article, "These regulations are passed by the Second National Representatives Conference of the Communist Party of China (16th to 23rd July, 1922) and are valid from the date announced by the Central Executive Committee." Whether this date was in the original Chinese document or whether Ch'en supplied it we cannot now be certain, since in other appendices there are parenthetical items almost certainly supplied by him.[42] However, we do have here a quite precise date for the Congress.

Ch'en opens his account by saying the party had grown from childhood to manhood through a year's struggle, experience and action, the reasoning power of the members had become less haphazard and more constructive and their plans for action less sporadic and more systematic. The conference issued a strong manifesto and made a systematic program based upon observation of the economic and political aspects of China which was far more analytic and synthetic than the plans of the first Conference during the movement's adolescent period. This is strikingly similar to the tone and content of the "Brief History," which says that the Party's position was much stronger than at the first Congress, the quality of the membership improved, and the Party was a great deal more experienced. Those who gathered for the second Congress, it says, were united in Marxist doctrine, platform and objectives and were all capable of dialectical reasoning. The Party Platform was passed as was a manifesto stating the Party's views on domestic and international problems, says the "Brief History."

What Ch'en says about the maturing of the Party in its first year seems correct. There is a completely different spirit as between the two documents resulting from the First Congress and the three passed by the Second which he provides. The Manifesto of the Second Congress is militantly anti-imperialist. The Decisions are much more detailed and specific than those of the First Congress, show a knowledge of the experience of European labor movements, repeatedly declare allegiance to the international Communist movement, and stress the need for a centralized and disciplined revolutionary party of the masses. The rules of organization are more elaborate and sophisticated than the naive rules from the First Congress; they stress centralized control and discipline.

Ch'en discusses some major decisions of the Congress, basing his account primarily upon Appendix 4, "The Decisions of the Second Conference of the Communist Party of China 1922." The Congress dropped the non-compromise policy in order to cooperate with the Nationalist Party, recognized the autonomy of Mongolia, Tibet and Turkestan, and "adopted parliamentary procedure" (by which Ch'en means the members were encouraged to seek seats in parliament and other assemblies). He then explains several points.

He explains the decision to "join the battle line" with the Nationalists by the argument that the proletariat must help the bourgeoisie to effect its stage of the revolution, the destruction of feudalism, before the proletariat can bring on Communism. The national revolution will benefit both the bourgeoisie and the proletariat. The Communists should unite all revolutionary parties to overthrow the feudal militarist party and imperialistic oppression and establish a democratic independent nation. They should lead the workers and peasants into the struggle under the Communist banner as the first step towards the establishment of their rights.

At the end of the chapter Ch'en speaks of an International Conference of Revolutionists summoned to Moscow at the end of 1921 and states that the change in Chinese Communist policy toward the Nationalists "is no doubt due to that conference." The Conference he refers to is the First Congress of the Toilers of the Far East, which held a preliminary meeting in Irkutsk in November, 1921; the delegates then traveled to Moscow and then to Petrograd. The Congress lasted from January 21 to February 2, 1922. It had representatives of both the Kuomintang and the Chinese Communist Party and was one of the places where Comintern strategy for China was pressed upon both the Communists and the Nationalists.[43]

Thus at the Tenth Session the delegates heard Safarov, a prominent specialist on the Eastern problem, deliver a statement which clearly foreshadowed the policy toward the Nationalists which the Second Congress of the Chinese Communist Party enunciated just six months later. Speaking of the Kuomintang, he said,

> ... I am convinced that, in order to come to an understanding between the Communists, on the one hand, and the revolutionary nationalists, on the other, it is absolutely necessary for both sides to know each other well. We know that the Party which is at the head of the South China Government is a revolutionary-democratic Party ... and we hope to fight side by side with this Party in the future. . . . We say: In colonial and semi-colonial countries the first phase of the

revolutionary movement must inevitably be a national democratic movement. We give our support to this movement, as such, to the extent that it is directed against imperialism . . . and will do so in the future, but, on the other hand, we cannot recognize this struggle as our struggle, the struggle for the proletarian revolution. . . .

* * *

In summing up, we may say that, in colonial and semi-colonial countries, like China and Korea, which are actually the colonies of foreign capital, the Communist International and the Communist Parties are obliged to support the national democratic movement. In these countries the Communist Party must advocate the overthrow of Imperialist oppression and support democratic demands such as the nationalization of land, self government, etc. At the same time, however, the Communist Parties must not abandon their Communist program, just as they must not abstain from organizing the working class in trade unions, independent of bourgeois influence. Neither must they abstain from organizing the working class in an independent Communist Party . . .[44]

Chang Kuo-t'ao was a delegate to the First Congress of Toilers, and presented a detailed report to the Chinese Communist Party's Central Committee. He recalls that the "Manifesto of the Second Congress" and the resolutions adopted at the Congress were drafted on the basis of the spirit and content of the resolutions of the First Congress of Toilers.[45]

These data support Ch'en's assertion that the change in Chinese Communist Party policy toward the Nationalists between the First and Second Congresses was due to the International Conference of Revolutionists.

Ch'en Kung-po lists the "demands" of the Communists for cooperation with the Nationalists. These are the well-known seven points, of which the last has six parts, set out in the Manifesto of the Second Congress.[46] A point of interest on which he remarks is recognition of Mongolia, Tibet and Turkestan as autonomous states, which might then be freely federated with China proper into a Republic. The status of Mongolia was at this moment a divisive issue between China and Soviet Russia. The Chinese government long claimed sovereignty over Mongolia and opposed Mongolian autonomy, which it regarded as a device for Russian encroachment. Chinese troops had been driven out of Urga by a White Russian army in February, 1921. Early in July the Mongolian People's Army and Red Russian forces had marched into Urga and on July 12 had established the Provisional People's Revolutionary Government of Mongolia. On November 5 representatives of the Mongolian People's Government and the Russian Socialist Federated Soviet Republic (R.S.F.S.R.) had signed in Moscow an Agreement for Establishing Friendly Relations. This reassertion of Russian power in Mongolia proved an obstacle to Soviet attempts during 1921-22 to establish official relations with the Chinese government.[47] Our Chinese Communist formula of autonomous Mongolian, Tibetan, and Turkestan states freely federating with the Chinese Republic would appear to be a device to avoid a touchy issue for Chinese nationalism.

Ch'en calls attention briefly to the decision that Communists should try to gain seats in parliamentary bodies, a reversal of the position of the First Congress. He then presents in turn the decisions reached regarding the Chinese labor movement, youth movement and women's movement. The Congress decided that the Party should redouble its activity in these fields. Since his remarks essentially restate what is found in the Decisions themselves, Appendix 4, I shall not rephrase Ch'en. Two things may be noted, however. In February, 1922, immediately after the First Congress of Toilers of the Far East, there were held in Moscow a Congress of the Revolutionary Youth of the Far East, and the First Conference of the Toiling Women of the Countries of the Far East.[48] Second, early in May, 1922, two months before the Second Congress of the Chinese Communist Party, the First Congress of the All-China Labor Federation, and the First Congress of Socialist Youth were held, both in Canton, and both under the guidance of the Communist Party. Ch'en was in Canton at the time of these meetings and probably was well informed about them. He gives a precise date, May 2nd to 6th, 1922 for "the first conference of the National Labor Union," mentions 160 representatives, and lists eight bills passed.[49]

To conclude, although Ch'en Kung-po did not attend the Second Congress, he gives a clear account of its major decisions and an adequate explanation of policy shifts.

1. **Documents of the Second Congress**

Ch'en gives three documents from this Congress. Two of them do not appear in any other source I have been able to find.

Appendix 3

"The Manifesto of the Communist Party of China adopted in July 1922 by the Second Congress" is a well known document in Chinese. I have compared it with a text re-issued by the Central Committee of the Chinese Communist Party in October, 1926 and with a version printed in 1930. Ch'en gives a faithful, sentence-by-sentence translation.[50]

There is, however, a difficult problem of its date. Ch'en captions it, as above, "adopted in July 1922 by the Second Congress." Whether this date was in the title of the version before him or was supplied by him is hard to say. It is also dated July in some Japanese sources.

However, in the official collection of Chinese Communist documents issued by the Central Committee of the Party on October 10, 1926, it is dated at the end in Chinese, "The Second Congress of the Communist Party, May, 1922." This source prints next the "First Manifesto of the Chinese Communist Party on the Current Situation," which it dates June 15, 1922.[51] Chu Ch'i-hua, an historian of Chinese communism, implicitly dates the

Manifesto of the Second Congress as May when he says that "about a month after this Manifesto the Party also issued its First Manifesto on the Current Situation." This he dates June 15, 1922.[52] This "First Manifesto" was indeed dated June 15; the original published text, issued by the Central Committee of the Chinese Communist Party on June 17, 1922, exists in the Library of Congress.[53]

The question at issue is whether the Manifesto of the Second Congress should be dated May or July, before or after the "First Manifesto" of June 15, 1922.

Miss Julie How and I dated the Manifesto of the Second Congress as May, 1922 and the First Manifesto on the Current Situation as June 15, based on the sequence of the documents and the dates given in the official CC collection of 1926, as well as on the differences between the positions the documents take on class alignments, and on the fact that only the First Manifesto of June 15 singles out the KMT by name as the potential revolutionary ally.[54] On the other hand, Chang Kuo-t'ao, reminiscing more than thirty years after the event, states that he worked on the drafting of the Manifesto of the Second Congress which consisted of the First Manifesto with important revisions.

There are several dating clues within the Manifesto of the Second Congress itself. One is the reference to the Genoa Conference.[55] This lasted from April 10 to May 19, 1922. Another is the reference to the civil war between Wu P'ei-fu and the Chihli faction and Chang Tso-lin and the Fengtien group in which Wu was victorious and won control of Peking. Control passed to Wu about May 4 or 5, though the fighting continued northeast of Peking until mid-June. The Manifesto treats this war as a matter of the recent past: "After the victory of Wu P'ei-fu, the Peking Government gradually drifted into the hands of pro-American bureaucrats, . . ."[56] The third clue is the statement, "Great Britain unscrupulously assisted the reactionary General Chen Chuen-Ming to overthrow Dr. Sun Yat Sen's Nationalist Power in Canton"; and a later statement, "Though the Canton government is now overthrown."[57] This seems clearly to refer to Ch'en Chiung-ming's coup d'état against Sun on June 16. If this is correct, the Manifesto of the Second Congress in the form we have it must date after mid-June. In fact the outcome of Ch'en's coup probably was not clear for several weeks, for Sun took refuge on a gunboat near Canton and his forces continued to contest for control of the city until early August. Furthermore, the labeling of Ch'en as a "reactionist general" seems to show that the Communist leaders had taken their stand against him—a stand they apparently did not take till July or even August when Sun arrived in Shanghai.[58]

On the basis of this internal evidence I believe the version of the Manifesto which Ch'en Kung-po translated as his Appendix 3 did date from late July. But there is always the possibility that a few sentences up-dating the text were inserted in printed versions, creating an inner anachronism. Dating by internal evidence is not necessarily conclusive.

Appendix 4

"The Decisions of the Second Conference of the Communist Party of China 1922" is an important document with a decided ring of authenticity. The men who wrote it had a much clearer understanding of Marxist theory, of Leninism, and of Communist Party principles and organization than did those who drafted the Decisions of the Party a year earlier. The document represents a milestone in the historical development of Chinese communism and deserves to be read carefully.

There are nine major sections or "decisions" on nine broad topics. Each begins with a categorical statement on existing conditions. The tone, in good Marxist style, is assertively confident of complete grasp of "the objective situation." Then comes a series of explicit guides to Party action.

The *first* decision concerns world conditions, describes Soviet Russia as the motherland of the world proletariat, and announces the decision of the CCP to call the oppressed Chinese masses to help protect Soviet Russia.

The *second* decisions concerns international imperialism, described as predatory towards China and the root of her difficulties. China can be united only when imperialism and feudal militarism are overthrown. The Party should unite the workers under its banner to fight for these goals.

Decision *three* concerns the "Nationalist Joint Battle Line." It provides a rationale in the theory of class struggle and the concept of historical development from feudalism through democracy to communism for the argument that the proletariat under the CCP should aid the national revolution. It includes the important injunction to the Party to maintain its organizational independence. There is an interesting statement, "The Second Conference of the C.C.P. approves the policy of joining the Nationalist joint battle line as proposed by the Central Executive Committee. . . ." This turned out to be one of the key decisions in the history of the Chinese Communist movement, though the subsequent decision that Communists should join the Nationalist Party itself was even more decisive.

The *fourth* is a brief announcement of the decision to become a branch party of the Communist International. The Congress accepts the 21 conditions of membership. These had been laid down by the CI at its Second Congress in 1920, and called for a tight, conspiratorial organization.

Decision *five* justifies members of the Party entering parliament to fight against militarism and imperialism. According to Ch'en, this was a reversal of the decision of the First Congress.

The *sixth*, on the Labor Movement and the Communist Party, is a most important section and bears attentive reading. It lays down nineteen fundamental policies based upon "the present condition of Chinese labor, our past activities and experience, and the result of discipline in modern European labor movements. . . ." These policies are sophisticated and intransigent; they lead towards revolution, not social reform.

Decision *seven* on the Youth Movement reads almost like an independent document. It gives a brief analysis of the position of youthful labor under capitalism and of the international proletarian youth movement; discusses the position of laboring youth in China; and then defines the relation between the Chinese Communist Party and "The Young Socialist Group." The CCP recognizes this Group as an "independent party" but states that "for purposes of a general political movement, the Young Socialist Group should always be controlled by the Chinese Communist Party." To ensure cooperation "the Conference recognizes the necessity of sending representatives from the various grades in each organization to confer with each other. How this should be done should be decided upon and carried out by the Central Executive Committees of those two parties."

Does this hint a conflict between the leadership groups of the two radical organizations?

The *eighth* decision about the Women's Movement is constructed much like the section on Youth. Apparently the Party had not yet gotten around to organizing women. However, in conformity with the instruction of the Third International that every national Communist Party should organize a committee to lead women, elect a women's department, and open a special column for women in communist newspapers, the Party "decided to adopt this plan as soon as it can."

Finally comes a decision on the constitution of the Party. Here we see the concept of a fighting party, leader of the proletarian revolutionary movement. "The one aim of those at the controlling center of the party should be to prepare and discipline their members so that they will be ready for revolution when the time is ripe." The party must be centralized, with iron-like laws, the members trained to almost military discipline and willing to sacrifice self for party.

Do we not hear the echo of Lenin in these decisions?

There are two dating clues in this document. One is a reference to the first national conference of the Young Socialist Group.[59] The Socialist Youth Corps held its first congress in May, probably beginning May 1, 1922.[60] The second is the statement that Wu P'ei-fu "intrigues to unite North and South by military means, and now reassembles the Old Parliament as an evidence of his good intentions...."[61] This seemingly refers to events between May 28, 1922, when Wu assented to the restoration of the Old Parliament and August 1, when a quorum of the 1917 Parliament began its meetings.

Appendix 5

"The Organization of the Communist Party of China" is the earliest constitution or statutes of the Chinese party available except for the primitive version of a year earlier given in Ch'en's Appendix 1. There is a relationship between the two. In Appendix 1, the rules of organization begin with numbers 4 and 5 which concern membership; these correspond to Chapter 1 on Membership in Appendix 5. The last item in Appendix 1, on method of amendment, corresponds to number 28, the next-to-last item in Appendix 5. There are several other resemblances.

However, it is evident that during the year which separates the two documents the Party had developed a more sophisticated system of organization, as we should expect. A Chapter of seven articles (4-10) is devoted to Organization. Aside from the primary group (properly called "cell") to which members normally belong, there are now three levels of organization: local, sectional, and central or national. In this hierarchy authority flows downward from central through sectional to local levels. Methods are specified for coordinating groups at the local and sectional levels through elected executive committees. Election of the Central Committee by the National Representative's Conference, length of tenure of committees at the various levels, and their duties are specified.

The third chapter (11-16) on Conference details the proper frequency of meetings of representatives at various levels and specifies who has the power to call conferences. The executive committee controls each level of organization. That power descends is made explicit in Chapter 4 (17-25) on Discipline. Between annual sessions of the National Conference of Representatives the Central Executive Committee has supreme powers; it can command and dissolve lower bodies. Local and sectional executive committees may not establish their own policies, nor speak on national issues before policy is set by the Central Executive Committee. Decisions of the National Conference and Central Committee are binding upon all members. The minority must absolutely obey the majority on all policy decisions. However, a majority in a group may protest to a higher level the decisions or actions of its own executive committee; means for settling such disputes are specified. Number 25 specifies the grounds and procedures for expulsion of a member. There is a brief Chapter on Revenue, which comes from dues, extra contributions within the party, and outside subsidy. The Central Executive Committee controls revenue and expenditures of the party.

The final rule, number 29, states that the regulations were passed by the Second National Representatives Conference of the Communist Party of China, which is precisely dated " (16th to 23rd of July, 1922) ". It states that the regulations become valid from the date to be announced by the Central Executive Committee.

What was the model for these regulations? Presumably it was the Rules (*Ustav*) of the Russian Communist Party which were adopted at the Eighth Party Congress, March 18-23, 1919, according to one source.[62] They were modified in some details in the Eleventh Party Congress, March 27–April 2, 1922, and again at the Twelfth Party Conference (sic) in August, 1922; but this would be after our document was composed. Other revisions followed periodically.

Despite extensive search I have been unable to find a copy of the Russian Party rules of a date prior to July, 1922 in a language I can read. Thus I must leave to someone else to determine the affiliation of the rules adopted at the Second Chinese Congress.[63]

Professor Hazard made the following comment after reading Appendix 5. "Not in any way a copy of the then existent Statutes of the Russian Communist Party (of Bolsheviks) then in existence as adopted by the 8th Conference [sic] (Dec. 1919).

"The concepts incorporated are, however, the same. Thus: structure of CP cells, hierarchy of organization, party discipline, revenue are the same as the Russian CP, but these are not expressed in the same words, nor are they identical in all detail.

"The impression is given that some draftsman, familiar with the Russian Statutes of the CP, made a set of rules for the Chinese CP, taking into consideration special circumstances in the Chinese Party, perhaps historical, of which I have no knowledge."

One point about these regulations may have a particularly interesting historical significance:

"22. Any member of the party, unless by special consent of the central executive committee, is not permitted to enter another political party or group. He who has been a member of any other political party or group, when entering our party, should formally resign from that party or group, unless he has the consent of the central executive party [sic] to remain in it."

The equivalent rule in Appendix 1, number 4, says: ". . . but before he enters our party, he shall sever relation with any party or group which opposes our program."

Thus, in July, 1922 the Central Committee had the power to consent to a member entering another political party or group, or to allow a new recruit to retain his membership in some other party. The significance is that very soon thereafter, in August, Chinese Communists began to enter the Kuomintag. A special plenum of the CC held in Hangchow in August, 1922, formally decided to allow Communists to join the KMT. This decision was taken, it is believed, because Sun Yat-sen, who arrived in Shanghai on August 14 after being expelled from Canton by General Ch'en Chiung-ming, rejected the communist proposal of an alliance between his party and theirs but agreed to admit Communists to the Kuomintang.[64]

Number 22 of Appendix 5 seems to show that the Communist leadership was itself ready for its members to penetrate other political parties even before Sun gave up the fight at Canton and returned to Shanghai. Another explanation for the existence of this rule could be that after the decision had been taken for Communists to join the KMT the rule was amended in the form available to Ch'en Kung-po.

D. *The Communists in Alliance with the Nationalists*

After Communists started to enter the Kuomintang a close relationship between the two parties began to develop. But the relationship was a gradually evolving one; its nature changed with the changing political fortunes of both groups and with their success in exploiting each other.

Ch'en Kung-po has some interesting observations on the earliest phase of this developing relationship. However, he was probably not personally involved since according to the biographical sketch given above, he had begun to detach himself from Communist affairs in the summer of 1922 and left for Japan in early November. His account of development after the Second Congress seems vague.

Chapter V of his essay is devoted largely to an exposition of Sun Yat-sen's ideas, based upon his book *The International Development of China* and the "Three Principles of the People." Ch'en, in his own words, regards Sun not as a "socialist but as a democrat," yet he also regards elements of Sun's program as leading towards the goal of state socialism. He explains the attitude of the Communist Party towards Sun's ideas and why communists entered his party. They regarded him as a nationalist rather than a socialist and joined his party from the viewpoint of nationalism and not of socialism. Ch'en supports this assertion by a quotation from the Decisions of the Second Congress, Appendix 4 (3), in which the Chinese Communist Party decides to join the national revolutionary movement in a temporary union to fight feudal militarism and imperialism, but does not surrender to the nationalists, who only represent the bourgeoisie.

He mentions the Communists' call to the Nationalist Party and the Young Socialists for a conference to work out plans for cooperation,[65] but apparently does not know whether such a conference was held. He states that the Communist Central Committee issued a proclamation in July, 1922, asking all its members to enter the Nationalist Party. I do not know of such a proclamation, and would be surprised if one to that effect were issued before the Hangchow Plenum in August.

Ch'en also says the Party simultaneously issued a manifesto to announce the reason and necessity for cooperation with the nationalist party, and that the Communist magazine "Forward" began propaganda for nationalism. He presumably alludes to the Manifesto adopted by the Second Congress, Appendix 3, which does argue the necessity for the proletariat and poor peasantry to assist the national revolutionary movement. *Hsiang-tao Chou-pao* [Guide Weekly] was established in September, 1922 as an organ of the Communist Party; one of its important themes was the necessity for the united front of all revolutionary groups. Perhaps Ch'en uses "Forward" as his translation for *Hsiang-tao*.

Ch'en Kung-po concludes Chapter V with a denial that Sun Yat-sen is a socialist or that he desires to make China "red." Publicity to this effect in the Western press apparently had nettled Ch'en; he insists that "nationalism is nationalism and communism is communism, and there is no chance for them to be intermingled." The Communists cooperate with the Nationalists because nationalism can improve the proletariat. No one, he says, can forecast the result of their cooperation.

He continues this theme in Chapter VI, asking how long and how far the Communists can cooperate with the Nationalists. The parties were originally distinct, he points out. The Nationalists represent the bourgeoisie and the Communists the proletariat; one recognizes the right of private capital and the other denies it; one accepts international capitalism while the other resists it. The Communists recognize the independence of Mongolia, Tibet and Turkestan while the Nationalists refuse to do so. The Communists advocate international revolution while the Nationalists' revolution is national only.

It was evident to Ch'en, writing in New York early in 1924, that the alliance was likely to be temporary. He cites the criticism of the Nationalists in the Manifesto of the Third Conference of the Chinese Communist Party (Appendix 6). He cites the strategy of the Communists in allying with the Nationalists in order to build up proletarian power; and their planned tactics when working in labor unions organized by Nationalists, Anarchists, or Christians to prepare to overthrow the original leadership.[66] "That these two parties will eventually split is very clear to the Communists," he says. [67] And he predicts that the Nationalists, when they succeed, will break with the Communists.

Ch'en says that the Third Conference of the Chinese Communist Party was held in July, 1923, in Canton where Dr. Sun's government was situated. The "Brief History" dates it June, and the Manifesto of the Congress appeared in an issue of *Hsiang-tao Chou-pao* for June 20, 1923.[68] It seems that Ch'en Kung-po, who was in America at the time of the Congress and no longer in the movement, was mistaken on the date, though only contemporary evidence would be conclusive.

Ch'en Kung-po concludes his thesis as he began it, with an attack on imperialism, the source of China's troubles. He criticizes the Paris Peace Conference of 1919 and the Washington Conference of 1921-22, the first for "butchering" China, and the second for failing to restore her lost rights. He supports his view with a long quotation from the Manifesto of the Second Congress of the CCP. Its anti-imperialist theme seems most congenial to his thought.

Appendix 6

"The Manifesto of the Third Conference of the Chinese Communist Party 1923" is the second of Ch'en's six documents for which a Chinese source is available. It was printed in *Hsiang-tao Chou-pao,* No. 30, June 20, 1923, p. 228. It has been translated and published in Brandt, Schwartz and Fairbank, *A Documentary History of Chinese Communism,* pp. 71-72. Ch'en's translation is a literal one, though the English words he uses for Communist terminology are not always the ones used today.

There are some divergencies from the *Hsiang-tao* text. Toward the end of the second paragraph Ch'en Kung-po has the Manifesto say ". . . these hardships fall heaviest upon the citizens, who, except through concentrating their own effort toward *the communist form of government* can find no other way to emancipate themselves." (my italics). The *Hsiang-tao* version says ". . . except through concentrating their own efforts toward a *powerful national self-determination movement . . .*". This crucial difference could be explained by the hypothesis that Ch'en had a different Chinese text before him which spoke of "the communist form of government" instead of the more palatable "national self-determination movement." The two expressions are so different in Chinese that the hypothesis of mistranslation seems unlikely.

I find untranslated one phrase about civil war instigated in Szechwan by Wu P'ei-fu and Hsiao Yao-nan, and a careless translation "social revolutionary elements" for "revolutionary elements in society." Ch'en translated Honan as Hunam, and his romanization system is somewhat erratic. There are doubtless other variations; Ch'en tends to be inaccurate even in quoting his own appendices. But except for the crucial point about the Communist form of government, the translation is adequate.

III. REFLECTIONS

It was exciting to discover in the Columbia Library Ch'en Kung-po's early history of Chinese Communism. The historian is interested in the truth about the past. Here is a nugget containing some truth in a field where subjectivity and revision of the past for reasons of present expediency is quite the order of the day. Ch'en's essay is important partly because it was written in 1924 and then was stored away for over thirty years, safe from the hands of revisionists.

The most valuable historical material is the four Appendices, 1, 2, 4 and 5. They appear to be authentic documents of the Chinese Communist Party, dating from its very first year. So far as I can determine they have not been available to other historians. Dating from the First and Second Congresses of July, 1921 and July, 1922, these documents give an insight into the early nature of the Party. They also provide clear evidence of its maturing.

The "First Program," actually a primitive constitution, is naive compared with the "Organization of the Communist Party of China," a constitution dating from the Second Congress. Simple though the latter is, it outlines a coherently organized, hierarchical, and disciplined party tied to the Communist International.

The contrast between "The first Decisions as to the objects of the Communist Party of China 1921" and "The Decisions of the Second Conference of the Communist Party of China 1922" is even more striking. The first gives no explicit theoretical basis for the decisions, and its six points for action provide very little detail. By contrast, the second set of decisions is shot through with Marxist and Leninist interpretation, while the lines of Party action are spelled out explicitly. We see clearly the intent that the Chinese Party, based in Marxist theory, should be a tightly organized and disciplined proletarian party, ready to join with other political groups in China for revolt against imperialism and militarism, but dedicated to a proletarian revolution thereafter. Even though the Party was in its formative stage, the change in one year is marked.

Because the Communist movement was secret and conspiratorial, and at first barely able to lodge itself against the opposition of Chinese and Western authorities, it seems to have left behind very few documentary traces of its early years. To find at this date four fundamental documents, long since believed by the Communists themselves to be lost, is not an inconsiderable event.

When he wrote this essay, Ch'en Kung-po was playing the role of historian. His position in Chinese political life was, temporarily, a somewhat detached one. He was outside the Communist movement but not yet in the Kuomintang. Nevertheless, he was much under the influence of the ideas which the Communists preached in 1922, and he was developing an interest in the reformist plans of Sun Yat-sen. These conclusions may be deduced from his essay but are supported by the available biographical and autobiographical information.

Ch'en was an ardent young nationalist. This comes through most clearly. His basic intellectual framework was the economic interpretation of history. He accepted the doctrine that imperialism was the root of China's problems. He also accepted the Chinese Communist Party's interpretation of its own existence—that "communism sprouts from the soil of foreign capitalism and imperialism." His explanation of why the Communists decided in 1922 to ally themselves with the Nationalists went back, probably unconsciously, to Lenin's theses on revolution in the colonial and semi-colonial countries, propounded at the Second Comintern Congress in 1920.

Ch'en was rather unoriginal in his explanations of modern Chinese history and the communist movement, for the most part simply quoting or paraphrasing his documents. Nor did he reveal much of his personal knowledge of the movement. He did not, for example, mention the name of a single Communist, though we know he was acquainted with most of the early leaders such as Ch'en Tu-hsiu, Li Han-chün, Chou Fu-hai, Chang Kuo-t'ao, Mao Tse-tung, T'an P'ing-shan, Chang T'ai-lei, and that he had met Maring and Joffe. His essay never hinted at Russian or Comintern assistance in the formation of the Communist Party though the later ties are not concealed. Ch'en alluded to certain controversies in the Party over policy but gave little detail and maintained a position of detachment even though we now know he was a partisan in some of the disputes. This reticence is easy to explain on the basis of loyalty to comrades and the discretion of a foreign student hiding the fact that he had been a founding member of a Communist Party.

The essay, while reticent about inside information, is still valuable for some details. For example, it provides three precise dates, July 20 for the opening of the First Congress in 1921, and July 16-23, 1922 for the dates of the Second. It dates the First Conference of the National Labor Unions as May 2-6, 1922. The first two events it locates in Shanghai and the third in Canton.

Ch'en clearly points out the relationship between the May 4th Movement of 1919 and the emerging Communist Movement. He explains the attitude of exclusiveness and hostility toward other political groups adopted by the First Congress in contrast to the policy of cooperation with the Nationalists adopted by the Second, and correctly attributes the change to the influence of the Congress of the Toilers of the East which intervened. His explanation why a Manifesto of the First Congress was never issued—because of disagreement over Party attitude toward Sun Yat-sen—is new information. There is considerable to be learned about the First Congress, if we read attentatively.

In sum, Ch'en Kung-po's essay and its documents are important for the history of the Chinese Communist movement, but only for its first organized year. They can tell us little about developments after July, 1922.

In reading the essay I was struck by Ch'en Kung-po as a prophet. Here are four of his predictions made in 1924.

At the end of his Introduction he says, "Though Chinese Communism is young, it has swept very rapidly over China. Whether it will take the same path as in Russia is questionable. . . . Human beings can improve their environment but they cannot entirely escape its influence upon their lives, so no matter how far the Chinese Communism succeeds, China is at last China, as Russia is Russia, and that the success of Communism in China will take a different form from that in Russia is my opinion."[1]

After recounting the growth of radical sentiment in China after the First World War, Ch'en says, "In a word, the old land of the Far East is now overflowing with radicalism. If the oppression in China does not cease, perhaps in the near future a new regime in China will trouble the historian to add a page to world history describing the further victories of Sovietism."[2]

On the cooperation between Communists and Nationalists, which was just being solidified under Borodin's guidance as he wrote, Ch'en observes, "The cooperation of those parties will surely be an important and a great change worthy of the future historian. Now those two parties are struggling in South China as well as in the North. Whether their program will be worked out will depend upon the patience of the two. . . ."[3] Nevertheless, Ch'en foresaw an inevitable split between them. "The split in their friendship will come sooner or later, but it is too early to say that it has begun now. When the Nationalists succeed they will break with the Communists. It is rash to forecast a sudden change. Time alone will tell us."[4]

Ch'en's final prediction is in the form of a quotation from the Manifesto of the Second Congress. He uses it to end his essay. "Three hundred millions of Chinese peasants are the important factors of our revolutionary movement. The peasants are in misery for several reasons—lack of land, density of population, prevalence of calamity, civil war and banditry, extra-taxes imposed by militarists, pressure of foreign commodities and the increasing cost of living. . . . If these poor peasants hope to escape from this miserable environment, there is only one way for them—that is revolution. And it is to be believed that the Chinese revolution will immediately succeed, when the majority of the peasants ally with the workers."[5]

When Ch'en Kung-po wrote these interesting predictions he was a thirty-one year old journalist studying in an American university. The next year he plunged into a political career that proved to be meteoric. Its tragic end two decades later prevented his seeing the fulfillment of all his predictions.

NOTES

I. The Author of the Essay

[1] The *Han Feng Chi* (hereafter cited as HFC) is a rare item. At the time of its publication, Ch'en Kung-po was one of the leading figures in the Nanking "puppet" government under Japanese protection. The work contains the following. Part I (314 pages) is largely autobiographical: "Recollections of My Childhood," written in 1935; "One Corner of My Life," 1933; "Fragments Recollected from the Army" (concerning the 'Northern Expedition' of 1926), 1936; "I and the Communist Party," 1943; "A History of the Reorganization Clique," 1944; and "Supplement to My Recollections of 1907," 1944. Part II (69 pages) is mostly literary: "My Poetry," "On Prejudice," 1943; "On Comprehension," 1943; "Friendship of the Poor and of the Rich," 1943; "Unadmirable Official Position," 1943; "Mayor of Shanghai," 1942; "Shanghai Peculiarities," 1943. The concluding note is signed October, 1944.

[2] Ch'en gave different birth dates on various times that he registered at Columbia. On the first occasion, February 28, 1923, he gave his birthdate as "28th August, 1891," in Canton. When he registered on September 27, 1923 he gave the birthdate as "September 29, 1891." When he registered for the last time in September 1924, he gave his birthday simply as "1892." See Columbia University, *Records of the Registrar*. Microfilm, Reel 3, Graduate Registration 1912-1926, Campbell to Cranston.

Several times in HFC, Ch'en gives his age in *sui* when particular events took place. If he was using the term to indicate his "Chinese age," according to which a child is two *sui* on the advent of his first lunar New Year, then Ch'en was born in 1892.

A member of the Ch'en family has informed me that Ch'en Kung-po was born on the 29th day of the 8th month according to the lunar calendar, in the year of the dragon, which was 1892. According to Pierre Hoang, *Concordance des chronologies néoméniques chinoise et européenne*, Shanghai, 1910, the 29th day of the 8th lunar month in 1892 would be October 19.

One may hypothesize that when Kung-po first registered at Columbia he knew his lunar birthdate to be the 28th or 29th day of the 8th month, and simply called the 8th lunar month August. On registering the next time he called it September. Why he gave the 28th one time and the 29th the next is a puzzle. He may also have been uncertain how to convert the reign year in which he was born.

³HFC, I, pp. 2-9 and 313. I am indebted to a member of the Ch'en family for the information as to its Hakka origin. Ch'en Kung-po does not mention in the reminiscences that he was a Hakka but he spoke the language freely. Both Shang-hang and Ju-yüan are in areas where Hakkas are concentrated. The account of the elder Ch'en's revolutionary activities appears in HFC, I, pp. 2-8, and pp. 284-314.

⁴Schooling: HFC, I, pp. 2, 11, 20-23. In his first registration at Columbia he listed "Kardomie [or Kardomi's] College, 1909-1913, Diploma." Life in Hongkong: HFC, I, p. 9.

⁵HFC, I, pp. 12-13, 24, 194-95. His Columbia registration says he was in Canton Law College from 1913-17, but in HFC he several times mentions his *three* years in the Law College.

⁶The outstanding work on the subject is Chow Tse-tsung, *The May Fourth Movement: Intellectual Revolution in Modern China*, Cambridge, Mass.: Harvard, 1960.

⁷HFC, I, pp. 196-97. Ma Hsü-lun, *Wo Tsai Liu-shih Sui I-ch'ien* [My Life Before Sixty], Shanghai, 1947, p. 124. Edgar Snow, *Red Star Over China*, New York, Modern Library, 1944, p. 150.

⁸Ch'en Kung-po, *The Communist Movement in China*, p. 76.

⁹HFC, I, pp. 197-98. One wonders whether the date of writing, 1943, when Ch'en was already collaborating with Japan made it politic to minimize his own involvement in the anti-Japanese aspect of the movement.

¹⁰HFC, I, pp. 200-203.

¹¹Chow Tse-tsung, cited, p. 248.

¹²HFC, I, p. 203.

¹³HFC, I, 204. According to "A Brief History of the Chinese Communist Party," an inside account composed probably late in 1926, Ch'en Tu-hsiu organized the Canton group and enlisted T'an P'ing-shan, Ch'en Kung-po and T'an Chih-t'ang after his arrival, thus differing from Kung-po's reminiscent account which has the organizations already underway when Ch'en Tu-hsiu arrived. See C. Martin Wilbur and Julie Lien-ying How, *Documents on Communism, Nationalism, and Soviet Advisers in China, 1918-1927*, New York: Columbia, 1956, pp. 50-51. Hereafter cited as Wilbur and How, *Documents*.

¹⁴HFC, I, p. 205.

¹⁵HFC, I, pp. 214-228.

¹⁶HFC, I, pp. 217-219. There is apparently a serious lapse here. "Slevelet" must be Sneevliet, the Dutch socialist who founded the first socialist party of Java, which soon became the Communist Party of Indonesia. He was expelled from Java and was for some years one of the Comintern's Far East experts using the name "Maring." Hugh Seton-Watson, *From Lenin to Malenkov; the History of World Communism*, New York, 1953, p. 135 n. 1 and 139, n. 2. Harold Isaacs, who interviewed Maring about his role in China, makes the same identification, *The Tragedy of the Chinese Revolution*, rev. ed., Stanford, 1951, p. 58, note. See also Robert North, *Moscow and Chinese Communists*, Stanford, 1953, p. 19. However, Maring, accord-

ing to many accounts, attended the First Congress of the Chinese Communist Party in Shanghai in July, 1921. See *Chung-kuo Hsien-tai Ko-ming Yün-tung Shih,* p. 100. Tung Pi-wu, a participant, says "Two delegates from the Comintern also attended this conference. One was from Holland—we call him Ma-lin in Chinese." Nym Wales [Helen Foster Snow], *Red Dust,* Stanford, 1952, p. 39. Ch'en Kung-po, also a participant, mentions seeing Maring at the aborted fourth meeting. HFC, I, pp. 206-08. Maring did visit Sun Yat-sen in Kweilin, probably on two occasions in 1921, in August or September and on December 25. See Wilbur and How, *Documents,* p. 139 and p. 497, n. 7 and 8. [This is incorrect. Dr. Sun was in Canton, not Kweilin, in August and September 1921. I am uncertain that he saw Maring then. He did confer with him in Kweilin about December 23-25, according to *Kuo Fu Nien P'u Ch'u Kao* (A Preliminary Draft Chronological Biography of the Father of the Country), Taipei, second printing, March 29, 1959, pp. 518-20. Added by CMW, August 1965.]

How could Ch'en Kung-po, who says he saw Maring at the First Congress, have failed to identify him as the "Slevelet" he met with Chang Chi in Canton? Assuming the account is factual, the following explanations seem possible: "Dr. Simon" may not have been Sneevliet; Ch'en only assumed this when he wrote. Kung-po may have forgotten, when he wrote more than 20 years later, that they were the same person. He may not have observed Maring distinctly at the aborted evening meeting in Li Han-chün's home (it was only a few minutes) and so did not recognize "Slevelet" as Maring. Sneevliet may have been disguised while traveling in South China as "Dr. Simon," so Kung-po failed to recognize him as Maring.

Chang Chi does not mention this incident in his complete works, *Chang Pu-ch'uan Hsien-sheng Ch'uan-chi,* Taipei, 1951. The work contains long passages of diary material, and an autobiographical sketch, but it should not surprise us that Chang's role in helping to bring the Kuomintang and Communist party together would not be mentioned since later he was one of the most vigorous opponents of inter-party organization. [This is incorrect. Although I have not found Chang's account of this particular incident, I have found—since writing the above—passages in which Chang Chi freely admitted his friendship for Maring and his role in introducing Maring to Sun. See work cited, pp. 195, 443, and *Chang Po-ch'uan Hsien-sheng Ch'uan-chi P'u-pien,* Taipei 1952, p. 109. Added by CMW, August 1965.]

[17]HFC, I, pp. 220-222. This passage is extensively quoted in Shen Yünlung, *Chung-kuo Kung-ch'an-tang chih Lai-yuan,* Taipei, 1959, pp. 17-18.
[18]HFC, I, p. 222.
[19]For an account of the revolt see Li Chien-nung, *The Political History of China, 1840-1929,* edited and translated by Ssu-yu Teng and Jeremy Ingalls, Princeton, 1956, pp. 415-19. Sun sailed for Shanghai about August 10.
[20]HFC, I, pp. 223-24. The meeting to reorganize the Kuomintang was held on September 4; see Wilbur and How, *Documents,* p. 141.
[21]HFC, I, pp. 225-27.

[22] Chen Pan-tsu [Ch'en T'an-ch'iu], "Reminiscences of the First Congress of the Communist Party of China," *Communist International*, American edition, Vol. 13, No. 10, October 1936, pp. 1361-66, p. 1362. Also in British edition, Vol. 13, No. 9, September-October, 1936, pp. 593-96 with slight differences in spelling and paragraphing. The romanizations all need to be corrected since they were transcribed through Russian into English. Chang Kuo-t'ao's account was taken, with permission, from the manuscript of his autobiography, Book 5, Ch. 3.

[23] Nihon Gaiji Kyokai, *Shina ni Okeru Kyōsan Undō* [The Communist Movement in China], Tokyo, 1933, p. 372. Gaimusho Jōhōbu [Foreign Office Information Bureau], *Gendai Shinajin Meikan* [Biographical Dictionary of Contemporary Chinese], Tokyo, 1928, p. 215. Hatano Ken'ichi, "Saishin Shina Jimbutsu Bankakyō" [Most Recent Biographies of Chinese Personalities], *Chūō Kōran*, No. 599, Vol. 52, No. 10, Special Issue, October 1937, Appendix, p. 19. I do not know what significance to put on the fact that General Ch'en and Kung-po were both Hakka with the same surname.

[24] Li Chien-nung, *op. cit.*, p. 419. Wilbur and How, *Documents*, p. 61. Chang Kuo-t'ao, *Autobiography*, Book 5, Ch. 3: Shen Yün-lung, cited, pp. 18-19, and 22-23, quotes various sources to indicate that Ch'en Tu-hsiu, himself, favored Ch'en Chiung-ming rather than Dr. Sun, and that he introduced Maring to General Ch'en in December 1921 before Maring saw Sun in Kweilin. Mr. Shen's work is inadequately annotated.

[25] After writing the above I received the interesting article by Professor Wu Hsiang-hsiang, "A preliminary investigation of Ch'en Chiung-ming's relations with the Russian and Chinese Communists," (in Chinese) in *Chung-kuo Hsien-tai Shih Ts'ung-k'an*, vol. 2, Taipei, 1960, pp. 97-118. While not dealing with Ch'en Kung-po's position, this well-documented study shows that before his coup of June 16, 1922, General Ch'en was courted by Maring and Ch'en Tu-hsiu, was praised by organs of the Comintern, advocated socialism and favored the organization of labor unions, and was apparently seriously considered by the Russians and the Chinese Communists as a possible ally.

[26] HFC, I, pp. 229-30. Ch'en gave much the same account of his conversation with Joffe in an article "Some Mistakes in the Nationalist Revolution," *China Weekly Review*, Vol. 44, May 26, 1928, pp. 398-402. It is also told in T'ang Liang-li, *The Inner History of the Chinese Revolution*, London, 1930, pp. 157-58; also in T'ang, *Wang Ching-wei: a Political Biography*, Peiping, 1931, p. 78. Joffe probably reached Japan at the end of January, 1923, which means Kung-po must have spent two months there before the Atami meeting.

[27] *Records of the Registrar, op. cit.*

[28] HFC, pp. 231-236.

[29] I have used the following sources in addition to HFC for Ch'en's later career:

Chia I-chün, *Chung-hua Min-kuo Ming Jen Chuan* [Biographies of Eminent People of the Chinese Republic], Peking, 1937, vol. 1, pp. 99-100.

Nihon Gaiji Kyōkai, cited, p. 372.
Tōa Mondai Chōsakai [Research Institute for Asian Affairs], *Saishin Shina Yojin Den* [Biographies of Recent Important Chinese], Osaka, 1941.
Gaimushu Jōhōbu, cited, p. 215.
Who's Who in China. Shanghai, Editions of 1928, 1931, 1933.
China Year Book, Shanghai, 1929-30 and later.
Who's Who in Japan, with Manchoukuo and China, 1940-41, Tokyo, 1941, p. 66, also pp. 35-37.
T'ang Leang-Li, *The Inner History,* cited.
T'ang Leang-Li, *Wang Ching-wei,* cited.
Ch'en recounts some personal experiences of 1925-27 also in:
"Some Mistakes of the Nationalist Revolution," cited; and "The So-called Left Wing," in Wang Ching-wei and others, *The Chinese National Revolution: Essays and Documents,* Tientsin, 1931, pp. 81-93.
In 1936 Ch'en wrote *Ssu Nien Ts'ung Cheng Lu* [Four Years in Government Service], which has a 120-page memoir of the period 1932-35 when he was Minister of Industry of the Nationalist Government.

[30] *China Yearbook,* 1929-30, p. 928.

[31] Ch'en Kung-po, *Chung-kuo Li-shih shang ti Ko-ming,* Shanghai, Futan Bookstore, December 15, 1928. 97 pages. I had hoped that this work would contain a Chinese text of his MA essay, or some of the documents, but it does not. He states on page one that his plan to make a new economic interpretation of Chinese history began in 1920 when he published a general outline in the Canton *Fa Cheng Hsueh-pao* [Journal of Law and Politics]. Then in 1924 at Columbia University he analysed the 1911 revolution, using only the economic background, and wrote a book in English, "China's Most Recent Social Movement" 中國最近的社會運動 . (It is interesting to speculate why Ch'en, in 1928, chose to conceal the true title and nature of his MA thesis.) Not till 1928, he says, did he have another chance to turn to his book, but even now because of shortage of reference books, his work is only an outline. According to Ch'en's definition of revolution—a movement combining economic collapse and violent action of the masses—there were true revolutions only in the Ch'in, Sui, Yuan and Ming periods. Accordingly he devotes a chapter to each of these periods, treating first economic collapse and then mass revolt. He does not come down to the Republican period.

II. The Essay on the Communist Movement in China

[1] A convenient summary of the official CCP list of the Congresses and account of their accomplishments is found in U. S. Consulate-General Hongkong, *Current Background* No. 410, September 25, 1956. The most useful of the articles it uses is by Pei T'ung in *Hsüeh Hsi,* September 1, 1952.

[2] Chen Pan-tsu, cited, pp. 1361-62.

[3] Helen Foster Snow, *Red Dust,* p. 39.

[4] Edgar Snow, *Red Star,* p. 157.

[5]Chou Fu-hai, *Wang I Chi* [Reminiscences], Shanghai, 10th ed., August 1944. Chou's reminiscences on early Chinese Communism are found in an essay, pp. 21-46, on his student days in Japan. My account is based on the notes of Mrs. Susan Han Marsh, to whom I am much indebted for allowing me to see them. Chou's account of the Congress is on pages 30-32. It is quoted at length in Shen Yün-lung, cited, pp. 10-12.

[6]*New York Times Magazine,* August 2, 1953, p. 46.

[7]This is based on the manuscript, Book II, Ch. 6, kindly made available by Mr. Burton. A much earlier work, "Communism in China," allegedly by Chang Kuo-t'ao, was seized in a raid on the Soviet Consulate in Canton in December, 1927, and a partial translation was published in the *South China Morning Post,* February 4, 1928. See Robert C. North, *Moscow and Chinese Communists,* p. 55, note 12. The item is available in the J. Huston collection in the Hoover Institute and Library, Stanford University. The account has some interesting information but is full of errors possibly due to poor translation; e.g., events of 1922 are all dated 1921.

[8]Wilbur and How, *Documents,* p. 52.

[9]Yu-Ang-Li, "The Communist International and the Foundation of the Communist Party of China." *Communist International,* American edition, vol. 6, nos. 9-10 [March-April], 1929, pp. 422-427, p. 425.

[10]Wan Min [Ch'en Shao-yü], "Fifteen Years of Struggle for the Independence and Freedom of the Chinese People." *Communist International,* British edition, Vol. 13, No. 9, September-October, 1936, pp. 581-93, pp. 581-582.

[11]HFC, I, pp. 205-12. Some of Ch'en's account is reprinted in Shen Yün-lung, cited, pp. 15-16.

[12]See below, p. 79.

[13]Chen Pan-tsu, cited, pp. 1362-64.

[14]Chou Fu-hai, cited, pp. 30-32.

[15]HFC, I, pp. 206-08.

[16]Helen Foster Snow, cited, p. 39.

[17]Chang manuscript, Book II, Ch. 6.

[18]Siao-yu [Hsiao Shu-tung], *Mao Tse-tung and I were Beggars,* Syracuse, 1959, pp. 198-203. The tale appears considerably embroidered. Particularly suspect are Hsiao's direct quotations of conversations which purportedly took place decades before, and also his claims to foresight. For example, p. 199, where, while walking from the train to Chiahsing, "I mused that these placid waters were so shortly to give birth to a monster, the Chinese Communist Party." And again, when he walks by the lake in the evening while the meeting is in progress, "I wondered which craft was destined to give birth to the Chinese Communist Party. The muddy waters of the lake made me think of the Deluge, the New Flood which would sweep away old China if the Communists were to dominate the country—turbid, murky, *huo shui* (evil waters)."!

[19]HFC, I, pp. 212-13.

[20]*North China Herald,* Vol. 140, Saturday, August 6, 1921, p. 407. The

recorded temperatures on July 30 and 31 were up to 99.2 and 96, and there was .08 inches of rain on July 31. *Ibid.* p. 448.

[21] From Ch'en T'an-ch'iu, Tung Pi-wu, and Chang Kuo-t'ao, all cited, we know that the delegates were Chang Kuo-t'ao and Liu Jen-ching representing the group in Peking; Teng En-min and Wang Chin-mei from Tsinan, Shantung; Li Han-chün and Li Ta from the group in Shanghai; Tung Pi-wu and Ch'en T'an-ch'iu from the Wuhan cities in Hupeh; Mao Tse-tung and Ho Shu-heng from Changsha in Hunan; Ch'en Kung-po and Pao Hui-seng representing Canton; and Chou Fu-hai representing Chinese comrades in Japan. Some confusion has arisen from differences in romanization. Chang Kuo-t'ao in the manuscript of his autobiography lists Pao Hui-seng as from Wuhan. We know from several sources that two Comintern delegates, Maring (pseudonym for Hendricus Sneevliet, a Dutchman) and Grigorii Noumovitch Voitinsky, a Russian, were on hand during the time of the Congress. Ch'en Kung-po mentions seeing them at the meeting that was interrupted by the police. He also says that Chang Kuo-t'ao relied upon the guidance of the two Russian delegates. HFC, I, pp. 206-207. Tung Pi-wu remembers their attendance but had forgotten the Russian's name. Chang Kuo-t'ao denies that either of them attended any meetings of the Congress and states that Maring was purposely excluded because two of the Chinese delegates disliked him. He was invited to the evening meeting at the home of Li Han-chün because he wished to speak to the Congress about the Constitution. This was the meeting interrupted by the police. Ch'en and Chang are at odds on several points and apparently grew to dislike each other intensely.

[22] Wilbur and How, cited, p. 53.

[23] Snow, *Red Dust,* cited, p. 40. I believe that Tung, in mentioning a "closed door" policy, was referring to the issue of whether members could belong to, or cooperate with, other parties or not. According to Kung-po's account the Congress decided "that no relation with other parties or groups is allowed," nor could they retain membership in other parties or groups. This debate is not mentioned by Ch'en T'an-ch'iu, Chang Kuo-t'ao, nor the "Brief History." Ch'en Kung-po elaborates in his reminiscent article written in 1943. He says he opposed the resolution but Chang Kuo-t'ao, who was chairman, insisted on its passage and the others simply went along. But at the next meeting Chang advocated rescinding the motion, on the advice of the Russian representatives. This incensed Ch'en who asked why there should be any Congress; why not just take orders from the Russians? HFC, I, pp. 206-207.

[24] Below, p. 82.

[25] Snow, *Red Dust,* cited.

[26] Chen Pan-tsu, cited, p. 1364.

[27] HFC, I, p. 207.

[28] Appendix 3: "Manifesto of the Second Congress of the Chinese Communist Party" in *Chung-kuo Kung-ch'an-tang Wu Nien Lai chih Cheng-chih Chu-chang,* 2nd ed., n. p. Central Committee of the Chinese Communist

Party, October 10, 1926, pp. 1-23. The volume is in the Library of Congress. (It is interesting that this collection of Party documents has none from the First Congress.) The Manifesto is also available in Chu Ch'i-hua (Chu Hsin-fan), *Chung-kuo Ke-ming yü Chung-kuo She-hui ko Chieh-chi* [The Chinese Revolution and Chinese Social Classes], 2 vols., Shanghai, 1930. Vol. 1, pp. 259-80. It leaves off the last paragraph and the slogans. The final section, without the slogans, appears in Nihon Gaiji Kyōkai, cited, pp. 95-97; a translation of this fragment is given in Conrad Brandt et al., *A Documentary History of Chinese Communism*, pp. 63-65.

Appendix 6: "Manifesto of the Third Congress of the Chinese Communist Party" is in the above Chinese collection of Party documents, pp. 45-47, and is found in *Hsiang-tao Chou-pao*, No. 30, June 20, 1923, p. 228. Also see Brandt, cited, pp. 71-72. A Japanese text is found in Rikugun Sambō Hombu, *Shina Kyōsantō Undō Shi* [A History of the Chinese Communist Movement], Tokyo, 1931, pp. 87-88.

29Wilbur and How, *Documents*, p. 52. Chen Pan-tsu, cited, pp. 1363-64; Chang Kuo-t'ao manuscript, cited; Chou Fu-hai, cited, p. 32; Tung Pi-wu in Snow, *Red Dust*, p. 40.

30HFC, I, pp. 208-11.

31Chen Pan-tsu, cited, p. 1363.

32*Ibid.*, p. 1366.

33Wilbur and How, *Documents*, p. 53.

34Eudin and North, pp. 84-85; 138-139.

35*Ibid.*, pp. 139-40, translated from B. Z. Shumiatsky. "Iz istorii Komsomola i Kompartii Kitaia (Pamiati odnogo iz organizatorov Komsomola i Kompartii Kitaia tov. Chang T'ai-lei)" [On the Communist Youth and Communist Party of China. In memory of one of the organizers of the Communist Youth and Communist Party of China, Comrade Chang T'ai-lei]. *Revoliutsionnyi Vostok*, No. 4-5, 1928, pp. 194-230, p. 216. Quoted by permission of Stanford University Press, publishers of Eudin and North, *Soviet Russia and the East, 1920-1927*.

36William E. Rappard, *Source Book on European Governments*, New York, 1937, Section V, "Government of Soviet Russia," by Samuel N. Harper, pp. V-7 to V-33. Also James H. Meisel and Edward S. Kozera, *Materials for the Study of the Soviet System: State and Party Constitutions, Laws, Decrees, Decisions and Official Statements of the Leaders in Translation*. 2nd rev. ed., Ann Arbor, 1953. No. 65.

37Wilbur and How, *Documents*, pp. 41-57, particularly pp. 54-57.

38U. S. Consulate-General, Hongkong, *Current Background*, No. 410, article by Pei T'ung in *Hsueh Hsi*, September 1, 1952.

39Wilbur and How, *Documents*, p. 60. The text may also be translated "when the Second Congress was about to close."

40*Ibid.*, p. 58. Pavel A. Mif, *Heroic China; Fifteen Years of the Communist Party of China*, New York, 1937, p. 14. Hua Kang, *Chung-kuo Min-tsu Chieh-fang Yün-tung Shih*, Shanghai, 1940. Reprint 1947, Vol. 2, p. B. 51.

A Documentary History, p. 30.

[41]Chang manuscript cited, Book 5, Ch. 3. Chang does not depend on his memory alone. He had many documents and historical works available.

[42]See below, pp 103, 122.

[43]Eudin and North, *op. cit.*, pp. 145-147, 221-231. Allen S. Whiting, *Soviet Policies in China, 1917-1924*, New York, 1954, pp. 78-86, presents a vivid account of the Congress as it dealt with Chinese problems.

[44]Eudin and North, cited, pp. 227-29. Quoted by permission of the publishers, Stanford University Press.

[45]Wilbur and How, cited, p. 492, n. 18. See also Mr. Chang's forthcoming memoirs. Whiting's careful study of the Congress and of Comintern reports on China during 1922-23 shows, however, a wide variety of opinion among Comintern leaders regarding the Chinese bourgeoisie, Sun Yat-sen, and the Kuomintang.

[46]The text in Brandt *et al.*, *Documentary History*, has been retranslated from a Japanese text, but corresponds well with Ch'en's version. See also Wilbur and How, *Documents*, p. 59 for the "Brief History's" closely similar text translated from the Russian back into Chinese and into English.

[47]Eudin and North, cited, pp. 121-30; Whiting, cited, pp. 155-78.

[48]Eudin and North, cited, p. 147.

[49]Below, p. 77.

[50]See above, pp. 53-54, n. 28.

[51]*Chung-kuo Kung-ch'an-tang Wu Nien Lai . . .*, cited, p. 23 and p. 39.

[52]Chu Ch'i-hua, cited, vol. 1, p. 280.

[53]*Chung-kuo Kung-ch'an-tang tui-yü Shih-chü ti Chu-chang* [Manifesto of the Chinese Communist Party on the Current Situation], n.p., Central Committee of the Chinese Communist Party, June 17, 1922. 14 pages. See Wilbur and How, cited, p. 575. The text differs from the version given in Brandt *et al.*, *Documentary History*, pp. 54-63, taken from a Russian journal. The Russian translation lacks (at their p. 59) a long section arguing the futility of various proposals for solving the problem of China's disunity.

[54]Wilbur and How, *Documents*, pp. 82-83, 493, n. 19, and bibliography, p. 575. We thus reversed the sequence of the two documents as given in the Brandt collection. The argument about singling out the KMT as a revolutionary ally cuts both ways: in June, before news of Ch'en Chiung-ming's coup against Sun reached the Central Committee, it might have regarded the KMT as an ally, but during July when Sun's fortunes were at a low ebb and he was isolated on a gunboat, the Communist Party might have been more vague.

[55]Appendix 3, below p. 110.

[56]Below, p. 112.

[57]Below, pp. 112, 114.

[58]See the interesting statement in the "Brief History," Wilbur and How, *Documents*, pp. 60-61.

[59]See below, p. 128.

⁶⁰According to the chronology in Brandt, cited, p. 30, and Peter S. H. Tang, *Communist China Today*, 2 vols., New York: Praeger, 1957-58, vol. 2, p. 4. Both chronologies have numerous errors.

⁶¹Below, p. 118.

⁶²Derek J. R. Scott, *Russian Political Institutions*, London, 1958, p. 137.

⁶³Comparison with the Constitution of the Communist Party of the Soviet Union adopted at the 14th Congress in December, 1925 shows important structural similarities. See Walter Russell Batsell, *Soviet Rule in Russia*, New York, 1929, pp. 699 and 735-54.

⁶⁴Wilbur and How, *Documents*, pp. 83, 140-41, and notes; Benjamin I. Schwartz, *Chinese Communism and the Rise of Mao*, Cambridge, 1951, pp. 40-45; Brandt, *et al.*, cited, pp. 52-53; Peter Tang, cited, vol. I, pp. 33-34. Chang Kuo-t'ao's autobiography in manuscript asserts that Maring maneuvered the calling of the Hangchow Plenum of the CC and insisted upon Communists joining the KMT because Sun would agree only to this form of cooperation. But he places the Hangchow Plenum early in August, *before* Sun's arrival in Shanghai. Within a few days after the Plenum, Ch'en Tu-hsiu, Li Ta-chao, Ts'ai Ho-shen, and Chang T'ai-lei formally joined the KMT in a ceremony over which Sun Yat-sen presided, according to Mr. Chang, who, however, was not then in Shanghai. Chang Kuo-t'ao manuscript, cited, Book 5, ch. 3.

⁶⁵Below, p. 121.

⁶⁶Appendix 3, pp. 115-116; Appendix 4, pp. 119-21, 124-26.

⁶⁷Below, p. 97.

⁶⁸Wilbur and How, *Documents*, p. 66; *Hsiang-tao Chou-pao*, No. 30, June 20, 1923, p. 228. June is the date officially accepted by Communist Party historians today; see U. S. Consulate-General Hongkong, *Current Background*, No. 410, cited.

III. Reflections

¹Below, p. 68.
²Below, p. 78.
³Below, p. 95.
⁴Below, p. 97
⁵Below, p. 101.

BIBLIOGRAPHY

Batsell, Walter Russell. *Soviet Rule in Russia.* New York: Macmillan, 1929.
Brandt, Conrad, Benjamin Schwartz, and John K. Fairbank. *A Documentary History of Chinese Communism.* Cambridge: Harvard University Press, 1952.
Chang Chi. *Chang Pu-ch'uan Hsien-sheng Ch'üan-chi.* [The Collected Works of Mr. Chang Pu-ch'uan]. Taipei: Chung-yang Wen-wu, 1951.
張繼，張溥泉先生全集
Chang Kuo-t'ao. *[Autobiography].* Unpublished manuscript, 1958.
_____. "Communism in China," *South China Morning Post,* February 4, 1928. [A partial translation of a document seized in the Soviet Consulate in Canton in December, 1927, and attributed to Chang.] In the J. Huston Collection, Hoover Institute Library, Stanford, California.
Ch'en Kung-po. *Chung-kuo Li-shih shang ti Ko-ming* [Revolutions in Chinese History]. Shanghai: Futan Bookstore, 1928.
陳公博，中國歷史上的革命
_____. *Han Feng Chi* [Collected Writings]. n.p., Ti-fang Hsing-cheng She, 1944.
寒風集．
_____. "The So-called Left Wing," in Wang Ching-wei and others. *The Chinese National Revolution: Essays and Documents.* Peiping: China United Press, 1931. pp. 81-93.
_____. "Some Mistakes in the Nationalist Revolution," *China Weekly Review,* Vol. 44, May 26, 1928, pp. 398-402.
_____. *Ssu Nien Ts'ung Cheng Lu* [Four Years in Government Service]. Shanghai: Commercial Press, 1936. 2nd ed., 1937.
四年從政錄．
Chen Pan-tsu [Ch'en T'an-ch'iu]. "Reminiscences of the First Congress of the Communist Party of China," *Communist International,* American edition, Vol. 13, No. 10, October, 1936, pp. 1361-66; British edition, Vol. 13, No. 9, September-October, 1936, pp. 593-96.
Ch'en Shao-yü [pseud. Wan Min]. "Fifteen Years of Struggle for the Independence and Freedom of the Chinese People," *Communist International,* British edition, Vol. 13, No. 9, September-October, 1936, pp. 581-93.

Chia I-chün. *Chung-hua Min-kuo Ming Jen Chuan* [Biographies of Eminent People of the Chinese Republic]. Peiping: Wen-hua hsüeh-she, 1933. 2 vols.
賈逸君，中華民國名人傳
The China Year Book. Shanghai: 1929-30 and later.
Chou Fu-hai. *Wang I Chi* [Reminiscences]. Shanghai: Ku-chin Publishing Company, 10th ed., August, 1944.
周佛海，往矣集
Chow Tse-tsung. *The May Fourth Movement: Intellectual Revolution in Modern China.* Cambridge: Harvard University Press, 1960.
Chung-kuo Hsien-tai Shih Yen-chiu Wei-yuan-hui. *Chung-kuo Hsien-tai Ko-ming Yün-tung Shih* [A History of the Modern Chinese Revolutionary Movement]. n.p., 3rd printing, 1940.
中國現代史研究委員會．中國現代革命運動史
Chung-kuo Kung-ch'an-Tang tui-yü Shih-chü ti Chu-chang [Manifesto of the Chinese Communist Party on the Current Situation]. n.p., Central Committee of the Chinese Communist Party, June 17, 1922. 14 pages.
中國共產黨對於時局的主張
Chu Ch'i-hua (Chu Hsin-fan). *Chung-kuo Ke-ming yü Chung-kuo She-hui ko Chieh-chi* [The Chinese Revolution and Chinese Social Classes]. 2 vols. Shanghai: Lienho shu-tien, 1930.
朱其華（新繁）．中國革命與中國社會各階級
Columbia University. *Records of the Registrar.* Microfilm, Reel 3, Graduate Registration 1912-1926, Campbell to Cranston.
Eudin, Xenia Joukoff and Robert C. North. *Soviet Russia and the East, 1920-1927: A Documentary Survey.* Stanford: Stanford University Press, 1957.
Gaimusho Jōhōbu [Foreign Office Information Bureau]. *Gendai Shinajin Meikan* [Biographical Dictionary of Contemporary Chinese]. Tokyo: Tōa Dubun Kai Chōsabu, 1928.
外務省情報部．現代支那人名鑑
Hatano, Ken'ichi. "Saishin Shina Jimbutsu Bankakyō," [Most Recent Biographies of Chinese Personalities], *Chuō Kōran*, No. 599. Vol. 52, No. 10, Special Issue, October, 1937, appendix.
波多野乾一．最新支那人物万華鏡
Hsiao Shu-tung [pseud. Siao-yu]. *Mao Tse-tung and I Were Beggars.* Syracuse: Syracuse University Press, 1959.
Hua Kang. *Chung-kuo Min-tsu Chieh-fang Yün-tung Shih* [A History of the Chinese People's Liberation Movement]. 2 vols. Shanghai: Tu Shu Publishing Company, 1940. Reprint 1947.
華崗．中國民族解放運動史
Isaacs, Harold R. *The Tragedy of the Chinese Revolution.* Rev. ed., Stanford: Stanford University Press, 1951.
Li Chien-nung. *The Political History of China, 1840-1929.* Edited and translated by Ssu-yu Teng and Jeremy Ingalls. Princeton: D. Van Nostrand Company, 1956.

Ma Hsü-lun. *Wo Tsai Liu-shih Sui I-ch'ien* [My Life Before Sixty]. Shanghai: Sheng-huo, 1947.
馬叙倫. 我在六十歲以前
"Manifesto of the Second Congress of the Chinese Communist Party," in *Chung-kuo Kung-ch'an-tang Wu Nien Lai chih Cheng-chih Chu-chang*. 2nd ed., n.p. Central Committee of the Chinese Communist Party, October 10, 1926, pp. 1-23.
中國共産黨第二次全國代表大會宣言. 中國共産黨五年來之政治主張
Meisel, James H. and Edward S. Kozera. *Materials for the Study of the Soviet System*. 2nd ed. revised. Ann Arbor, Michigan: G. Wahr, 1953.
Mif, Pavel A. *Heroic China; Fifteen Years of the Communist Party of China*. New York: Workers Library Publishers, 1937.
Nihon Gaiji Kyōkai [Japanese Foreign Affairs Society]. *Shina ni Okeru Kyōsan Undō* [The Communist Movement in China]. Tokyo: Nihon Gaiji Kyōkai, 1933.
日本外事協會. 支那に於ける共産運動
North, Robert. *Moscow and Chinese Communists*. Stanford: Stanford University Press, 1953.
Rappard, William E. *Source Book on European Governments*. New York: D. Van Nostrand Company, 1937.
Rikugun Sambō Hombu. *Shina Kyōsantō Undō Shi* [A History of the Chinese Communist Movement]. Tokyo: Rikugun Sambō Hombu, 1931.
陸軍參謀本部. 支那共産黨運動史
Schwartz, Benjamin I. *Chinese Communism and the Rise of Mao*. Cambridge: Harvard University Press, 1951.
Scott, Derek J. R. *Russian Political Institutions*. London: Allen & Unwin, 1958.
Seton-Watson, Hugh. *From Lenin to Malenkov; the History of World Communism*. New York: Frederick A. Praeger, 1953.
Shen Yün-lung. *Chung-kuo Kung-ch'an-t'ang chih Lai-yuan* [The Origins of the Chinese Communist Party]. Taipei: Min-chu chao-she, 1959.
沈雲龍. 中國共産黨之來源
Siao-yu see Hsiao Shu-tung.
Snow, Edgar. *Red Star Over China*. New York: Modern Library, 1944.
Snow, Helen Foster [pseud. Nym Wales]. *Red Dust: Autobiographies of Chinese Communists*. Stanford: Stanford University Press, 1952.
Tang Liang-li. *The Inner History of the Chinese Revolution*. London: George Rutledge and Sons, Ltd., 1930.
_____. *Wang Ching-wei: a Political Biography*. Peiping, 1931.
Tang, Peter S. H. *Communist China Today*. 2 vols. New York: Praeger, 1957-58.
Tōa Mondai Chōsakai [Research Institute for Asian Affairs]. *Saishin Shina Yōjin Den* [Biographies of Recent Important Chinese]. Osaka: Asahi Shimbun Sha, 1941.
東亞問題調査會. 最新支那要人傳

U.S. Consulate General, Hongkong. *Current Background.* No. 410, September 25, 1956.
Wales, Nym see Snow, Helen Foster.
Wan Min see Ch'en Shao-yü.
Whiting, Allen S. *Soviet Policies in China, 1917-1924.* New York: Columbia University Press, 1954.
Who's Who in China. Shanghai: China Weekly Review. Editions of 1928, 1931 and 1933.
Who's Who in Japan, with Manchoukuo and China, 1940-41. Tokyo, 1941.
Wilbur, C. Martin and Julie Lien-ying How. *Documents on Communism, Nationalism and Soviet Advisers in China, 1918-1927.* New York: Columbia University Press, 1956.
Wu Hsiang-hsiang. "Ch'en Chiung-ming yu O Kung Chung Kung Kuan-hsi Ch'u T'an" [A Preliminary Investigation of Ch'en Chiung-ming's Relations with the Russian and Chinese Communists], in *Chung-kuo Hsien-tai Shih Ts'ung-k'an,* vol. 2. Taipei: Cheng-chung Bookstore, 1960, pp. 97-118.

吳相湘．陳烔明與俄共中共關係初探．中國現代史叢刊．第二冊．

Yu-Ang-Li. "The Communist International and the Founding of the Communist Party of China," *Communist International,* American edition, Vol. 6, Nos. 9-10 [March-April], 1929, pp. 422-427.

THE COMMUNIST MOVEMENT IN CHINA

by

Kung-po Ch'en

CONTENTS[1]

INTRODUCTION:	Fundamental Economic Changes in China	63
CHAPTER I	The Real Cause of the Chinese Revolution of 1911	69
CHAPTER II	The Forerunners of Chinese Communists	74
CHAPTER III	The First Conference of the Chinese Communist Party 1921	79
CHAPTER IV	The Second Conference of the Chinese Communist Party 1922	83
CHAPTER V	The New Program of the Nationalist Party and Its Recent Tendency	90
CHAPTER VI	The Third Conference of the Chinese Communist Party, 1923, and Conclusion	96
APPENDIX 1	The First Program of the Chinese Communist Party 1921 (translated from Chinese)	102
APPENDIX 2	The First Decisions of the Chinese Communist Party 1921 (translated from Chinese)	103
APPENDIX 3	The Manifesto of the Chinese Communist Party 1921 [1922] (translated from Chinese)	105
APPENDIX 4	The Decisions of the Chinese Communist Party 1922 (translated from Chinese)	117
APPENDIX 5	The Regulation of the Chinese Communist Party 1922 (translated from Chinese)	131
APPENDIX 6	The Manifesto of the Chinese Communist Party 1923 (translated from Chinese)	135
BIBLIOGRAPHY		137

[1] There are no footnotes in the original essay. All footnotes and all material in brackets have been supplied by the Editor, C.M.W. A few corrections have been made in Ch'en Kung-po's typing and spelling, but not his grammar. The wording of Ch'en's Contents does not always exactly correspond with his chapter headings and titles of Appendices.

INTRODUCTION

Fundamental Economic Changes in China

During the stress and strain of war, Russia passed from black autocracy to the Soviet Republic; Hungary followed suit, only to be forced back into temporary Hapsburg control by the force of the allied armies; Germany and Austria bade farewell to their strong monarchical governments and became republics presided over by socialists, and pressed increasingly by the demands of the masses for complete socialization of industry. In Great Britain, the British Labor Party at the end of the war became the chief opposition party in Parliament, bent on a complete reconstruction of the present industrial order, with the labor movement more unified on its industrial side. In fact, in every nation where capitalism had obtained a foothold, the struggle of the masses for industrial democracy, for socialism, during this period, gained increased momentum. Within the socialist movement a significant shift was evidenced in every country towards a more radical position than that held prior to the war. China has also been affected and although far behind other countries economically, must join forces with communism.

What China becomes now will be the result of capitalism. "There is, commonly, a handsome margin of profit in doing business with these pecuniarily unregenerate populations", explains Thorstein Veblen in the "Theory of Business Enterprise", "particularly when the traffic is adequately backed with force. But also commonly, these people do not enter willingly into lasting business relations with civilized mankind. It is necessary, for the purpose of trade and culture, that they be firmly held up to such civilized rules of conduct as will make trade easy and lucrative." Ever since the capitalist trade entered China, alas, China has become one of the victims of colonial policy and lucrative traffic.

The entry of imperialism into China began with the aggressive acts of the British fleet in 1839, a most piratical action. The underlying cause was the determination of the British government and merchants to poison the Chinese people with opium.[1] This "opium war" did not begin without sharp criticism from some quarters. One Dr. Arnold wrote to a friend, "Ordinary

---

[1] These two sentences and the next paragraph are taken from the Manifesto of the Second Congress of 1922; see below, Appendix 3, p. 107.

wars of conquest are to me far less wicked than to go to war in order to maintain smuggling, and that smuggling consisting of the introduction of a demoralizing drug which the government of China wishes to keep out, and which we, for the lucre of gain, want to introduce by force."

During eighty years of increasing foreign power, China, as a matter of fact, has become the colony of stronger nations. The imperialists not only occupy the broad territories, islands and protectorates as new colonies, but have robbed China of many important harbours in order to create foreign settlements and at last have divided China into several spheres of influence in order to further exploit her. In China, one-third of the railways are owned by the foreign capitalists, others are also directly or indirectly controlled by foreign creditors. Foreign steamers freely navigate in Chinese harbors and rivers, postal and telegraph services are closely supervised, and the tariff is dependent—controlled by the foreign imperialists. Under such a regime it is not only convenient for the foreigner to import their capital, absorb raw materials, but, worst of all, the soul of Chinese economic life is mercilessly clutched in the imperialist claw. The foreign capitalists also occupy many mines, they have established factories in Shanghai and Tientsin, and drive the Chinese workers with whips in the mines and factories as their productive slaves. At the same time the imports of foreign commodities rise like a relentless tide. The old home-made needles and nails are obliged to give way to the imported ones. The disastrous effect is the rise in the cost of living. Three hundred millions of peasants tend to become paupers, ten millions of handicraftsmen gradually become the proletariat. Cash indemnities were demanded of China at the end of every war. The compound interest of $2,000,000,000 upon foreign loans, and the control of foreign bankers in Shanghai, Peking, Tientsin, Hankow and Canton, affected the economic life of the nation, and the people are sorely harassed. The imperialists also bribe the bureaucratic politicians, send many advisers and missionaries to China, publish newspapers, and establish schools, all of which are only contrivances to spread imperialistic propaganda. They also secure consular jurisdiction privileges, and station their armies, police, and fleets in the territory of China.

This condition is described in the Chinese communist manifesto which points out that communism sprouts from the soil of foreign capitalism and imperialism. In order to make this monograph a complete and logical whole, I wish to give a sketch of the economic influences upon which the growth and tendency of Chinese communism are based. In the opinion of many, the economic interpretation of history does not consider the forces of socialism. Today, as Professor Seligman points out "The writers who are . . . making the most successful application of the economic interpretation are not socialists at all," but the profound influence of economic forces no intelligent man will deny and it has taught us to search below the surface, as Professor Simkhovitch says. We are quite prepared to admit that, and we will start from this point of view.

Concerning the growth of communism in China, we cannot deny what the Chinese communists state. We wish, however, to discern and understand what has maintained China for so many centuries on a low plane of material well-being, and has secured for her such prolonged ages of internal peace. All may be summed up in the Chinese devotion to agriculture on a small scale, with direct personal ownership of the soil they cultivate; the continuance of handicrafts; the partial influence of the customs of old village communities and the permanent sanctity of family life. The maintenance of agriculture and its fostering as the basis of all prosperity, and by far the most important national industry and business, were the foundations of the whole life of people. Since China's wall was battered down by the heavy artillery of cheap foreign commodities, the people have become miserable under the pressure of capitalism and imperialism.

The opium war with Great Britain in 1840, the war with Britain and France in 1856, with Japan in 1894 and the Boxer Rebellion in 1899, increased the indemnity to more than $529,640,000, and other loans amounted to not less than twice the indemnity. But the most fatal blow to China is the necessity of permitting leased territory. The theory of the international balance of power was and still is working in the Far East, particularly in an independent and sovereign but economically and militarily weak nation like China. In 1898, when Germany, on the pretext of the accidental murder of two German missionaries in a certain district of the province of Shangtung, demanded and secured the lease of Kiao-chow Bay for ninety-nine years from the Chinese Imperial government, Russia demanded and secured the lease of Port Arthur and Dalny for twenty-five years; France that of Kwang-chow Bay for ninety-nine years; Great Britain that of Kowloon for ninety-nine years to counterbalance France in the South, and that of Wei-Hai-Wei for twenty-five years to counterbalance Germany and Russia in the North. In 1905, the Russian leased territories in China passed into the hands of Japan. As the result of the late war, the German leased territory in China also passed into the hands of Japan, in spite of China's protest at the Versailles Peace Conference in 1919.

By lease is meant the transfer of title within a stated period of time, the lessee to pay a certain sum or rent to the lessor per annum or otherwise. Although China's sovereignty is not surrendered, she gets no rent nor can she impose any tax on the properties and the persons within the leased territory; these properties and persons are only subject to taxation by the governing or leasing power. It was in the Kiao-chow leased territory that Germany made the first successful experiment with the unearned increment tax. Even the customs revenues at Kiao-chow were not entirely China's, twenty per cent had to go to the German government in the leased territory. Since Japan seized it in 1914, China has been further deprived of the proceeds of the customs. What has been true of Kiao-chow has also been true of all the other territories in China.

Less humiliating to China than the leased territories are the "foreign concessions" or settlements at the so-called "treaty ports". The meaning of such a concession or settlement is the granting of permission by the Chinese government to the foreigners concerned to set up and maintain local administrative agencies for public purposes, such as sanitation, the making of roads, providing building regulations, etc. The administrative organs thus created levy taxes, the proceeds of which must be wholly devoted to the performance of these local administrative tasks. They may not be levied for any other purpose and the Chinese government has no share in them. Although some form of land tax in certain settlements is still collected by the Chinese government, China's right not only of general taxation but also of tariff imposition has come to naught in such concessions or settlements. China at present can tax neither foreign products nor Chinese goods in such special areas for foreign trade and residence beyond what is allowed by the treaties.

Thus no chance is given to China for fiscal reform. The only way the government can pay the capital and interest of foreign loans is to tax the people to the last extremity; it must kill the goose to obtain the golden eggs. The people are burdened by the heavy tax on one side, and exploited by the influx of cheap commodities on the other, and gradually they become paupers. In order to resist the oppression of foreign capitalism, the Chinese bourgeoisie begin to rise up, but as their power is so weak and their capital so small they only become the toys of foreign capitalists; as to competition with foreign capital, it is out of the question. What they can do or are obliged to do is to oppress the working classes and to reduce wages though the cost of living rises day by day. The result is that since the entry of foreign powers the handicraftsmen, small shop-bosses, and petty employers are becoming either bankrupt or losing their occupations. The women have to leave their comfortable homes to work in factories getting far lower wages than the male workers, while even the children are obliged to earn their living by monotonous machinery work for over fifteen hours a day. The condition of China today resembles the misery of England during the eighteenth century directly after the industrial revolution.

The bourgeoisie know nothing of labor legislation; and dreams of sanitary equipment never disturb foreign or Chinese bosses in their sound and comfortable sleep. The penal law even considers strikes criminal and gives no voice in politics to the laboring class. Partly due to the Great War, the cost of living has risen more than two hundred percent, but the standard of wages remains what it was twenty years ago.

The Chinese thought the revolution of 1911 would emancipate them from economic and political pressure, but because of the influence of foreign capitalism and imperialism, the misery remained, increasing from bad to worse. No matter whether China is a republic or a monarchy, the foreign capitalists still push on their lucrative traffic. Dissatisfied with the results of the revolution, and believing its effects insufficient to get rid of the oppression, the Chinese decided that another step should be taken—communism should be tried. While the Chinese people struggled to seek a new way of emancipation, the Red Army succeeded in Russia. The dynamite of radical thought exploded, communism swept over China, the labor classes united, strikes spread all over the country, intelligent students went among the workers, and the social revolution started on the way to success sooner or later. In a word, the seed of social revolution has been sown in the minds of the people, how long before it blooms depends upon the radical gardeners' energy.

We shall now discuss the recent tendency of the Chinese communist party. We are interested to read, on the last page of Marx's and Engel's Communist Manifesto, "In France the communists ally themselves with the Social Democrat. In Switzerland they support the radicals. In Poland they support the party that insists on an agrarian revolution as the prime condition for national revolution. In Germany they fight with the bourgeoisie whenever it acts in a revolutionary way. In short, the communists everywhere support every revolutionary movement against the existing and political order of things. In all these movements they bring to the front, as the leading question in each case, the property question, no matter what its degree of development at the time. Finally they labor everywhere in all countries...." They openly declare that their ends can be attained only by the forcible overthrow of all existing social conditions. So the communists of China have adopted this point of view and are trying to fight for a national revolution.

At the first conference of 1921, the Chinese communists adopted the policy of non-compromise, and recognized that in all parties in China were corrupt elements. "We should cut off all relations with the yellow intellectual class and other such classes. We should stand by ourselves. We should struggle independently. We should avoid becoming the puppets of other parties," they cried.[1] But a year later at the second conference they dropped their first program, and tried to cooperate with the Nationalist Party. "Every fact and event proves," declares the second manifesto "that what gives the Chinese people (whether bourgeois, worker or peasant) the greatest misery, is the force of capitalistic imperialism and of the militarist and bureaucratic feudalism. The revolutionary movement of nationalism opposes those two forces. Comparative liberty may be secured, when the national revolution succeeds. We, the proletariat, observing the existing Chinese political and economic conditions, advocate that we, the proletariat and the poor peasants, should assist the national revolutionary movement. We believe that during struggle, there is only one way to secure a national revolution . . . that is, by cooperation of the proletarian revolutionary forces and the national revolutionary forces."[2] In solving the problem of why the communists allied themselves with the nationalists, we should consider several points worth stating. In the first place, China is a backward country economically, very different from the western nations. Modern socialism is the result of indus-

---

[1] Part of the quotation comes from Appendix 1, point 3; also Appendix 2, Item (5).
[2] Appendix 3, below, p. 115

trialism, which has played an important role for two centuries in western history. Economic change, taking hundreds of years in other countries, takes place in a few years in China. Nationalism fails in China because it ripens too early. If communism also proceeds at too rapid a pace it will fail also. Secondly, China is republic only in name; the remnants of feudalism have not been swept away. Democracy is indispensable as a means of ripening a proletariat for the social revolution. Democracy, besides not being capable of preventing this revolution, is to the proletariat what light and air are to a physical organism. Without them, it can not develop its powers. Thirdly, China is very different from Russia. The latter is an absolutely independent country, and the former has been a semi-colony since the middle of the nineteenth century. All important ports are occupied by the Powers, economic life and politics are controlled by foreign imperialists, all activities limited by disadvantageous treaties. In addition, the army is weak, and the power of the fleet is naught. If the social revolution broke out, whether it would be profitable to the Powers or to the Chinese is still a question. It is also obvious that such a revolution would be met with force as in Hungary, or suppressed by the militarists, assisted by the foreign imperialists, as was the case with Denikin and Seminoff in Russia.

Whether my diagnosis is correct or not the communists have their own reason for dropping their first program of "isolated action". As a conclusion of this chapter, I want to add a few more words. Though Chinese communism is young, it has swept very rapidly over China. Whether it will take the same path as in Russia is questionable. As E. A. Ross states, "If the train bearing Lenin and eighteen other Bolsheviks across Germany to Russia had fallen through a bridge on its way and all had perished, events in Russia would have taken much the same course." Human beings can improve their environment but they cannot entirely escape its influence upon their lives, so no matter how far the Chinese communism succeeds, China is at last China, as Russia is Russia, and that the success of communism in China will take a different form from that in Russia is my opinion.

CHAPTER I

The Real Cause of the Chinese Revolution in 1911

As we want to logically present the growth of communism in China, we shall commence by stating that its birthplace is to be found in foreign imperialism and capitalism. China is in the position of a semi-colony as described in the first chapter; with the exception of a few missionaries and a few scholars, writers and artists who admire Chinese civilization, the interest of the world in general is a money interest pure and simple. So long as the capitalists in the industrial countries require and demand that these backward countries be exploited, humanitarian laws will not be allowed to interfere with the main economic purpose in these colonies and weak nations. Besides the entry through military force in the past, the foreigners now are eager to build railroads in China, not because they think the Chinese need railroads, but because the foreigners need the profit from the railroads. This then is a point of supreme significance, namely: that the fundamental aim of all the treaty stipulations and agreements as to intercourse, customs, extraterritoriality, spheres of interest, railway concessions and control is not the welfare of the people of China but the profit and ease with which the people of the West can carry on business.

To get rid of this economic pressure is a question of life and death to China, and the revolution of 1911 was the first step taken by the Chinese to free themselves. The overthrow of the Manchurian government, which seems to superficial observers to be caused only by race hatred, is really based upon economic causes. The following tables support this conviction.

INDEMNITY AND WAR LOANS

Title and Source	Principal Amount	Interest %
Hongkong and Shanghai loan (British)	10,000,000 pounds	7
Hongkong and Shanghai loan (British)	3,000,000 pounds	6
The French-Russian loan	400,000,000 francs	4
The Cassel loan	1,000,000 pounds	6
The Nanking loan (German)	1,000,000 pounds	6
The Anglo-German loan	16,000,000 pounds	5

INDEMNITY AND WAR LOANS (Continued)

Title and Source	Principal Amount	Interest %
The Anglo-German loan	16,000,000 pounds	4.5
The Boxer Indemnity	450,000,000 Taels	4

RAILWAY LOANS

Title and Source	Principal Amount	Interest %
Franco-Belgian loan (for the Peking Hankow Railway)	4,500,000 pounds	5
British and Chinese Corporation loan (for making the Imperial Railway of North China)	2,300,000 pounds	5
Russo-Chinese Bank loan (for the Shanghai Railway)	1,600,000 pounds	5
Franco-Belgian loan for the Kaifengfu Honan Railway	1,000,000 pounds	5
British and Chinese Corporation loan for the Shanghai Nanking Railway	2,250,000 pounds	5
British and Chinese Corporation supplementary loan for the Shanghai Nanking Railway	650,000 pounds	5
Pekin Syndicate loan for the Taokow-Chianghua Railway	700,000 pounds	5
Hongkong Government loan for the redemption of the Canton-Hongkong Railway	1,100,000 pounds	$4\frac{1}{2}$
British and Chinese Corporation loan for the Canton-Kowloon Railway	1,500,000 pounds	5
Anglo-German loan for the Tientsin-Pukow Railway	3,000,000 pounds	5
Anglo-German loan for the Tientsin-Pukow Railway	2,000,000 pounds	5
British and Chinese Corporation loan for the Shanghai-Hangchow Ningpo Railway	1,500,000 pounds	5
Anglo-French loan for the redemption of the Peking-Hankow Railway	5,000,000 pounds	5

RAILWAY LOANS (Continued)

Title and Source	Principal Amount	Interest %
Japanese loan for the Kirin-Changchun Railway	2,150,000 Yen	5
Anglo-German Supplementary loan (Tientsin-Pukow Railway)	3,000,000 pounds	5
London, City, and Midland Bank (Yuchuanpu Bonds for the Peking-Hangkow Railway Expenses)	450,000 pounds	7
Peking-Hangkow Railway Redemption loan (Yokohama Specie Bank)	220,000 Yen	7

GENERAL LOANS

Title and Source	Principal Amount	Interest %
The Ili Expedition loan	1,000,000 pounds	unknown
The Formosa Expedition loan	2,000,000 Taels	8
The South-West Expedition loan	5,000,000 Taels	15
The First Naval loan (German)	2,500,000 Marks	5 2/3
The Second Naval loan (British)	16,000,000 Taels	7
The Third Naval loan (German)	5,000,000 Marks	5
The Austria Munition loan	300,000 pounds	6
The First Austrian loan	2,000,000 pounds	6
The Second Austrian loan	1,200,000 pounds	6
The Currency loan	10,000,000 pounds	5
The First Cable loan (The Eastern Extension and the Great Northern Telegraph Company)	210,000 pounds	5
The Second Cable loan (The same source)	48,000 pounds	5

PROVINCIAL LOANS

Title and Source	Principal Amount	Interest %
The Chihli loan of 1905	4,800,000 Taels	7
The Hupeh loan of 1909	2,400,000 Taels	7
The Anhwei loan of 1910	1,200,000 Taels	7
The Hunan loan of 1910	1,200,000 Taels	7
The Hupeh loan of 1909	500,000 Taels	7
The Shanghai loan of 1910	3,500,000 Taels	4

PROVINCIAL LOANS (Continued)

Title and Source	Principal Amount	Interest %
The Shanghai Merchants' loan of 1910	2,000,000 Taels	7
The Kiangsu loan of 1910	3,000,000 Taels	7

The result was that just before the revolution of 1911, the total amount of loans was 82,448,000 pounds, 7,500,000 marks, 600,000,000 francs, 2,690,000 yen, and 502,000,000 taels. This total more than equalled 1,650,000,000 Chinese dollars, and the interest amounted to nearly 800,000,000 dollars, to be paid yearly. This unbearable burden was laid on the shoulders of the Chinese and was such a bitter yoke to them that they of course tried to find a way to remedy this unbearable state of affairs. In addition the government tried to do its best to modernize the country to walk in the steps of the Japanese who had succeeded so well in their dealings with foreigners. New institutions were formed, a new army trained, colleges and schools opened— every method used to raise the country to the rank of Western Powers. To meet the new expenditures brought by these changes everything that could be taxed was taxed to the limit. Besides the foreign loans carried by the people, they had to bear another tax burden for the reform of the nation. But China had no chance to reform, as the tariff was controlled by foreigners in the security of loans, and bounded by the conventional tariff, so that no tax could be increased. The products of Chinese handicraft were displaced in the market by foreign manufactured commodities. All the important ports were occupied by foreign capitalists. Lacking other means of emancipation the Chinese turned to revolt.

The revolution became an assured fact, and within one hundred days, the Manchurian government was overthrown. Fortunately the republic rapidly succeeded, and unfortunately the republic succeeded too rapidly. The government of the nation changed from a monarchy to a republic, and a parliament and cabinet were formed. All the various political systems of Europe were imitated in China, but the economic condition remained the same; no change came with the republic. Concessions and settlements were the same, the government could not tax or make any progress in fiscal reform, the customs were controlled by the foreigners, the factories and railways were managed by foreign capitalists, and even some privileges were ceded secretly in exchange for recognition of the Republic of China. In a word, the economic condition went from bad to worse.

Economic imperialism does not aid a republic. The economic ruin of China which began under the monarchy has been completed under the Republic. Instead of helping the new republic to get upon its feet, Europe and Japan have continued the system of economic exploitation. Civil war has been fomented and fostered by foreign loans, and this state of affairs has permitted the Chinese to squander money on their armies or to take the simpler and more direct course of putting money for the armies straight into their own pockets.

As the people still bore the heavy burden of taxation, unrest spread throughout China. Thus two extreme points of view arose. The conservatives thought that weighing the misery existing under a republic and under a monarchy, it were better to restore the monarchical system which was probably in practice better than the Republic. The radicals, on the contrary, advocated that what in the republic had been proved unsatisfactory could be remedied by turning their thoughts towards anarchy.

But what China wanted was peace rather than freedom. As Metternich was the power after the French revolution, so Yüan Shih-k'ai, the reactionist, soon became powerful. He put down the Nationalist Party, dissolved parliament, and finally tried to convert China into a monarchy with himself as emperor. After his death the republic was restored, but within a year, the Manchurian emperor was restored, only to be defeated in a month. What the conservatives recommended has been tried out in every particular, first, the new monarchy, then the restoration of the young puppet, the ex-emperor, which failed, and now the dream of monarchy dies away. On the other hand, the nationalist party is not fully successful, for several reasons. First, the revolution is, as a matter of fact, a fruit which has ripened too early. About two-thirds of the people do not quite understand what a republic means, especially those people of the North. Secondly, the remnant of feudalism has not been swept away, and those who opposed democratic methods in the time of the monarchy, have become powerful in the republic. Finally, the foreign capitalists and imperialists always are willing to give assistance to the conservatives so that democracy may be put down and their own special privileges furthered. First they helped by granting loans to the reactionist Yüan Shih-k'ai, then to the militarist party of the North. The most notorious conservatives these were, the greater help could they secure from foreign imperialists. Even the good term "open door" is only a phrase which really means the invading of China. No one can be more plain spoken than Mr. W. E. Weyl in explaining this policy, "Our interest in the matter, however, is frankly selfish. Though we have a kindly feeling for the Chinese, so long as they stay in China, our "open door" policy is intended in the first instance to benefit our own merchants and investors." What is true of the "open door" policy of America is also true with regard to the imperialistic plans of other powers.

What we have just described explains the success and subsequent failure of the political revolution of China in 1911. Where conservatism fails, radicalism will succeed. Where imperialism penetrates, communism begins. Before we discuss the first conference of the Chinese communists, it is well for us to discuss those men who began this movement.

CHAPTER II

The Forerunners of the Chinese Communists

The forerunners of the Chinese communists are hardly known to either foreign or Chinese writers. Though many expressions of ancient Chinese philosophers may be regarded as communistic, they can scarcely be considered a background for the recent movement. In *Socialism in Thought and Action,* H. W. Laidler states that "The first socialist organization in China was founded in 1911. During the Chinese revolution the movement spread rapidly and some thirty socialists were elected to the parliament of the New Chinese Republic. This success led to the establishment of more than two score socialist newspapers, to free socialist schools and labor unions, to the widespread distribution of socialist literature and to the socialist theatrical companies. Yüan Shih-k'ai, in August 1913, fearful of the result of their propaganda, issued an edict dissolving the party, arresting its leaders and jailing and executing many of them. The socialists, however, continued to conduct a secret propaganda, and were an important factor in the overthrow of the Yüan Shih-k'ai imperialistic government and the establishment of a new republican regime under Li Yüan-Hung." And Kirkup states the same thing in the *History of Socialism.*

But so far as I know, the socialist movement of 1911 was a kind of utopian scheme unrelated to the practical movement of today. At that time, there were two groups who advocated socialism and anarchism. The first had no platform or program but was an ordinary club without any relation to labor unions, and none of its members agitated the labor questions. Some socialists were elected to parliament, but they were listed in the Nationalist Party and not as belonging to the socialist party. The latter claimed nothing, and only advocated the "principles of public property and free love", and once petitioned the Canton government to grant them an island on which to realize their ideal "new community". With such idealistic thought we had better regard them as utopians rather than communists. So as we trace back the origin of the communist party, it is more practical for us to portray the Movement of May 4th, 1919, the prologue of the college students' movement.

After the armistice of the World War, the weak and oppressed nations expected a realization of their dreams of self-determination and independence, as promised by the Great Powers during the war emergency. Not until the curtain of the stage at Versailles fell, did these nations realize that what they had longed for would remain a dream. The fourteen points of Wilson failed of adoption, the promises of the Powers were broken, the masks of justice, equality, and humanity were put aside, and a new imperialism created by Clemenceau and Lloyd George began to flourish. No advantage in this new order of things could be secured for China, even the Shangtung problem could not be settled. China was kept out of the secret meetings of the five powers—Chingtau, the Bay of Shangtung was granted to Japan under the so-called "gentlemen's diplomacy of Great Britain," and with the understanding and acquiescence of the Great Powers. On May 4th, 1919, the college students of Peking National University and other colleges made a great demonstration before the foreign legations, demanding that the Powers relieve China from oppression. At the end of the demonstration they openly attacked the traitors Ts'ao Ju-lin, the minister of foreign affairs who signed the document containing the Japanese twenty demands, and Lu Tsung-yü and Chang Tsung-hsiang, the former and present Chinese ministers in Japan, who signed the papers of the Shangtung Railway loan from the Japanese government. They beseiged Ts'ao Ju-lin's house and beat Chang Tsung-Lsiang almost to death, while Ts'ao and Lu under the protection of the police fortunately escaped. More than thirty students were arrested, universities were put under military guard, martial law was declared, and more than two thousand students suffered arrest subsequently. As the jails were not big enough for all these students, the university buildings were temporarily used as prisons and surrounded by policemen and soldiers. What a terrible and wonderful scene it was! The gendarmes patrolled the roads and streets, the students made speeches to the crowds of soldiers armed with guns and swords. Some of the students were struck and whipped by the soldiers, but hundreds and hundreds of them continued their propaganda and public speeches incessantly and vigorously. The number of students was far more than could be arrested, no more rooms in the prisons and temporary jails could be found, the government was powerless to deal with the students, and at the end of this farce, the gendarmes did not imprison the students, but only confiscated their circulars and pamphlets, and drove the public who happened to attend their lectures out on the roads, and permitted the students to make their speeches only in the streets. But in order to prevent disorder, the imprisoned students still remained in the jails. Representatives of the Peking students were sent to various provinces which echoed everywhere with the slogan, "Down with the traitors. Oppose the Japanese and World Militarism." Throughout the whole Chinese nation a general strike of students took place. Several thousand young men returned to their homes telling the story of the outrage. Meetings were held in the class rooms, revolutionary resolutions were passed by the students throughout the whole country, and they refused to attend lectures. The merchants and the intellectuals, oppressed by the power of Japan and crushed by the militarist party, sympathized with the students, and strikes were planned to take place in such important ports as Tientsin, Shanghai, Hangkow, etc., if the demand that the traitors, such as Ts'ao Ju-lin, the minister of foreign affairs, Chang Tsung-hsiang, the minister to Japan, should not be dismissed and the imprisoned students released. The government, fearing a coup d'état, was obliged to set all the students free, to expel the two ministers, and the revolutionary storm was temporarily calmed.

Since then, this picturesque movement has created a great sensation among the Chinese people, shaking them from their apathetic drowsiness. This movement seems to be of a rather anti-Japanese character. The ardent believers in the revolution consider it a harbinger of an approaching storm.

The public has learned, and the progress of imperialism had made more clear, that the powers at the Paris Conference, throwing off their hypocritical masks under which they advocated peace without annexation or indemnity, planned to punish China as if she had been an enemy rather than an ally. Though the Chinese representatives did not sign the Versailles Treaty, Shangtung was held by Japan, and the dreams of the Chinese for solving the problems of tariff, consular jurisdiction, and foreign settlements did not come true. China was treated as were the Balkan countries, which are waiting to be redivided by the five Great Powers.

Thousands and thousands of young men, driven by radical thoughts, conscious of the weakness and corruption of the government, knew that the only way to release China from oppression was to depend upon self-reliance. "Go among the people" was the slogan.

Many of the students gave up their attendance upon lectures and went into the factories to organize labor groups and to foment strikes. Girl students formed the Women's Rights Movement Association, demanding the equality of the sexes in such matters as inheritance, political rights, education, the abolition of polygamy and girl slaves. Many of the People's Schools were organized by students to teach the workers both during the day and evening, and most of them even worked among the laborers in order to prepare them for revolutionary organizations. These movements were sporadic in character, but all tended toward the social revolution.

It is very interesting and stirring for me to recall my memories of this period. I was in the midst of the great wave, witnessed the radical movement from beginning to end, the deepening of dissatisfaction among the masses, and the stiffening of resistance. How much in beauty and sorrow this picture resembled the general strike of the college students of Russia in the winter of 1898-99!

Since the May 4th movement, many a party and group were organized. The following list show the sources from which the communists were drawn:

1. The Young Socialist Group. Like the First International this group was composed of various radical young men such as socialists, anarchists, syndicalists, utopians, and communists. After several severe arguments and discussions, the anti-communists retreated. Now this group has become purely communists.

2. Labor unions. Except one, all of these might be termed national—the National Labor Union. Hundreds of them are sporadic, mostly trade union in character. The power of the union is far less than that of similar unions in Europe, but their influence increases from day to day. They believe that China should follow in the footsteps of Soviet Russia.

3. Renascence Group. This group was organized during the stay of Professor John Dewey and Mr. Bertrand Russell in China. Professor Dewey advocated experimental logic and Mr. Russell preached guild socialism, but they both taught the students how to think. Now many communists come from that group, and the way we think and the results of our thinking have influenced the communist party. This is perhaps unknown to Professor Dewey and Mr. Russell.

4. The Marxian Club. The object of organizing this institution was to study Marxism. It was not a revolutionary but an intellectual group. Many of Marx's books were translated, but as the members of this club soon realized that only to understand the Marxian theory could not satisfy their ardent desires, they gradually turned to practical applications. Today about ninety percent of them have become communists.

5. The National Students Association. It escaped the oppression of the Peking government and flourishes in Shanghai. The object of the Association is to oppose Japanese imperialism. The deputies are elected by various provincial students, and most of them sympathize with radicalism and social revolution.

6. Women's Rights Movement Alliance. This organization has spread over China and is composed of school girls. Most of them believe that no complete emancipation of women can be realized unless Soviet China succeeds.

Among these organizations, the Young Socialist Group and the National Labor Union are the strongest organizations and are most actively working for the revolution. The Young Socialist Group has made its program, and in its first conference in 1922, it settled upon many policies concerning politics, economics, education and its relation with the other parties. The first conference of the National Labor Union met in Canton, May 2nd-6th, 1922, with more than 160 representatives, and eight bills were passed, namely:
1. A bill to assist the strikes
2. A bill urging the eight hour day
3. A bill concerning the principles involved in organizing the National Labor Union
4. A bill concerning the murder of Hunan workers by the Hunan government
5. A bill stipulating the use of a certain Chinese labor song and labor banner

6. A bill to respect May Day and punish the traitors among the workers
7. A bill to organize an association of coolies throughout the whole country
8. A bill to provide for the next national conference of labor unions

Except the above-mentioned parties which we regard as the parent organizations, many other organizations contain radical thinkers. In a word, the old land of the far East is now overflowing with radicalism. If the oppression in China does not cease, perhaps in the near future a new regime in China will trouble the historian to add a page to world history describing the further victories of Sovietism.

CHAPTER III

The First Conference of the Chinese Communist Party, 1921

The first Chinese Communist Party Conference of national representatives assembled in Shanghai on the 20th of July, 1921. It was the birth of the Communist Party of China. At the conference there were twelve deputies representing seven sections—Canton, Peking, Hunan, Shanghai, Shangtung, Tientsin, Hangkow, and the Chinese comrades in Japan. This conference lasted two weeks, and five committees were elected to draft the platform, program and manifesto.

In order better to understanding this conference, several significant points influencing the thoughts of the communists must be kept in mind. First, the civil war, prolonged from 1918, caused unbearable misery to the people. Secondly, as the Paris conference closed, imperialism and capitalism had made more clear to the whole world that the weaker nations had no chance to escape the control of the greater powers. The dream of the people of oppressed nations for emancipation could never become true, the oppressed classes of all countries must continue to suffer from the capitalistic governments. Thirdly, the Shangtung problem still was not settled, although the Chinese representatives had refused to sign the treaty of Versailles; Chingtau was in the hands of Japan as a donation of the great powers in spite of the protestations of the Chinese, and in spite of the aid rendered by China in the Great War as one of the Allies. Fourthly, under such conditions of oppression, it seemed not only to the radicals, but to the moderate intellectuals that there was no other way for them to emancipate China from internal and external oppression except through an immediate social revolution. As a result, all the members attending the conference advocated that the policy of "no compromise" should be adopted.

The important decisions[1] were as follows:

(1) With the revolutionary army of the proletariat, to overthrow the capitalistic class; to reconstruct the nation from the laboring class.

(2) To adopt the dictatorship of the proletariat in order to complete the end of class struggle—no classes.

(3) To overthrow the private ownership of capital, to confiscate all the means of production, such as machines, land, building, semi-manufactured products, etc., and to entrust them to social ownership.

---
[1] From Appendix 1.

(4) To unite with the Third International.

Because the social revolution was to be international, they abolished all discriminations due to nationality or sex in membership. Any one who believed in the platform and objects of the party and endeavored to be of service to the party might be a member of the party. They organized the workers, peasants, and soldiers and adopted the formulae of the soviets. In order to uphold the non-compromise policy, they decided to cut off all relations with the yellow non-communists.

In the first program,[1] they decided upon several policies to be undertaken concerning labor organization, propaganda, labor supplementing schools, institutions for studying labor organization and their attitude towards the other existing parties.

To form industrial unions, they recognized the aim of their party. The party should imbue the labor unions with the spirit of the class struggle. As to the existing guilds, technical unions, the party decided to send members to join these organizations in order to take the first step toward reorganizing those unions. But to accomplish their "non-compromise" policy, they vowed to avoid becoming the puppet of other non-communist parties also facing political struggles. In order to assume the dictatorship in propaganda, they decided that all magazines, daily publications, encyclopedia and pamphlets should be put under the management and direction of the Central Executive Committee. No publication was allowed inconsistent with the decisions and policies of the party.

The labor supplementary schools they regarded as a preparatory step in organizing the labor unions. When organized, they should be formed within the unit of a kind of industry, such as transportation and textile supplementary school, etc. The object of these schools was to establish gradually a center of labor organization, one side to foster revolutionary ideas on the other; the subjects taught should be those that would awaken the consciousness of laborers and show them the need for organizing labor unions.

Some sort of an institution was necessary to train workers in revolutionary ideals. The objects of the institution were to discipline the workers preparatory to putting their ideals into practice, to teach them how to organize labor unions and to investigate labor conditions. The institution was divided into various groups to study the history of labor movement, the method of organizing factory laborers, Karl Marx's theory and the present aspects of the labor movement in various nations.

A special stress had been laid upon their attitude toward other existing parties. "Towards the existing political parties," the program[1] ran, "an attitude of independence, aggression, and exclusion should be adopted. In the political struggle, in opposition to militarism and bureaucracy, and in demanding freedom of speech, press and assembly, our party should stand in behalf of the proletariat. No relation with the other parties or groups is

---

[1] Actually, the first Decisions, Appendix 2.

allowed." They laid special stress on this point for several reasons. In the first place as the civil war had endured many years, the people were in deep misery and depression, which made the communists believe that any party which caused such misery to the people was an enemy to them. The prolongation of civil war was terrible, and not only the Peking government but the government of the South is responsible. This made manifest the truth that neither existing party in China was worth joining. Secondly, many communists of the time represented the radical elements in other parties or groups. If they retained membership therein, the personality of the members would be demoralized. Thirdly, as the policy of non-compromise was the only policy they recognized, independent struggle was important for the party; it was no use for the communist to work with the non-communist.

Finally, the whole party decided to enter the Third International. Every month a report was made by the central committee to the Third International, of which, if necessary, the representative would be sent to the Far East Secretariat at Irkuchika.

This decision represented the period when the Communist Party was first being organized in China and it is interesting to observe that the communist point of view changed rapidly before the conference held the next year.

When the first conference closed, all the deputies left Shanghai, and returned to their own provinces for organization and propaganda. At the end of 1921, the Central Executive Committee was organized in Shanghai, acting more or less openly, and the provincial executive committees were reported to be established over half of China. Labor organizations were organized all over the country, especially in Canton where more than one hundred and twenty unions were formed and, although sporadic and like trade unions in character, they were gradually turning toward communism. Strikes occurred incessantly in the important ports of which the Seamen's Strike in Hongkong was known throughout the world, and gave the Hongkong and British government a great shock.

Before concluding this chapter, two or three more interesting things are probably worth mentioning.

In article fourteen of the party's program, they forbid the members to be officials and members of the various assemblies, and further explain that the principals of schools and presidents of colleges, if appointed by the government, were to be considered as officials, as indicated above. This evoked a bitter debate. The opponents of this measure held that the educational vocation should not be regarded as official service, and in addition that while the party was young, the members should be active where they could be, no matter in what professions they were, even in governmental positions. As the upholders of this side of the argument refused to be convinced, this provision was reserved for decision in the next conference.

Another important point was the failure to issue the first manifesto. The manuscript of the first manifesto was divided into two parts. The first part described the political and economic condition of China, basing its findings upon the theory of Marx and Engel's Communist Manifesto, and urging the need of a social revolution in China. The latter part enumerated the evils of the North and the South government, and stated that the government of Dr. Sun Yat-sen was no better than the government of the northern militarist party. This caused a fatal debate in the conference. Some of the members argued that though many wrong points of view were represented in the Nationalist platform, it more or less represented the new tendency for the time being. The principle of general welfare advocated by Dr. Sun resembled state socialism. On the other hand, a majority of the members held that because many of the Nationalists opposed the communists, the South government should be overthrown. The manifesto was passed at last, but another bill was decided upon the following day leaving the question of the issue of the manifesto to the decision of the Central Executive Committee. After the first conference, no issue of the first manifesto was distributed, and the manuscript of that manifesto is now not known to the world. The first conference was almost cut short by the police before it could begin to function.

At the end of the first week of conference, many bills were still under consideration and discussion, when the police agent suddenly appeared. Before the assembling of the conference many reports were received in the headquarters of the foreign concessions that a conference of the Oriental communists would meet in Shanghai, including Chinese, Japanese, Indian, Koreans, Russians, etc. All the concessions were secretly guarded, especially the French settlement. Perhaps because of a warning from some spy, detectives and policemen surrounded the conference building, but fortunately ten of the deputies warned the others of the danger, and fled. Even with four hours' search, no evidence was obtained, and the policemen retreated. In order to prevent the repetition of such an interruption the conference was held in a boat in the middle of a famous lake beyond the jurisdiction of the police, and many furious and radical decisions were made in the beautiful junk surrounded by peaceful and picturesque scenery, but the fiery feelings of the deputies were neither moderated by the pleasant calm water nor the beautiful moonlight.

CHAPTER IV

The Second Conference of the Chinese Communist Party, 1922

The second national representatives conference of the Chinese Communist Party was held in Shanghai in July 1922. Through a year's struggle, experience and action, the party had grown from childhood to manhood, the reasoning power of the members had become less haphazard and more constructive, and their plans for action had become less sporadic and more systematic. More than eighteen provinces sent representatives to this conference, and the conference issued a strong manifesto and made a systematic program based upon observation of the economic and political aspects of China, far more analytical and synthetic than those plans of the first conference, which might be criticized as the period of adolescence of Chinese communism.

In the program and decisions of the second conference, several significant features should be called to the attention, as this program and these decisions were contrary to what had been decided at the first conference. The second conference dropped the non-compromise policy in order to cooperate with the Nationalist Party. It recognized the autonomy of Mongolia, Tibet and Turkestan because of their different economic conditions. It adopted parliamentary procedure, which the first program did not allow. In a word it showed a great change in its policies and a great change in the history of Chinese communism. Perhaps some one will make the criticism that not communism but only moderate socialism prevailed in China, so that in order to have a clear understanding of this change, it is worth while for us to make the following detailed illustration.

(1) Why did the communists decide to join the battle line with the Nationalists?

To explain why they allied themselves with the Nationalists, the minutes[1] of the second conference state: "The economic and political evolution of human beings naturally constitutes the class struggle. During the period between feudalism and democracy, because of the economic and political changes, it is inevitable for the bourgeoisie to fight against feudalism. In like manner, during the period of the change from democracy to communism, it is also inevitable for the proletariat to challenge the bourgeoisie.

---
[1] Actually, Decisions. See Appendix 4, p. 119. The quotation is not exact.

The history of humanity is a record of struggle. The great war waged by the proletariat against the bourgeoisie is still not at an end, and that of democracy against feudalism is still raging. Especially in Oriental nations, young in their industries, the power of feudalism still exists in social traditions as well as in national sovereignty. Within those nations the lives and property of the people are firmly grasped in military hands, and the force of laws and public opinion upholds this state. For the common welfare it is necessary for the democrat to overthrow feudalism. If the proletariat can not bring on the revolution alone, they must be assisted first to fight feudalism. The feudal militarist party is the joint enemy of proletariat and democrat.[1] No freedom of the press, meeting or assembly is secured, unless these two classes unite, and no class can secure the opportunity to develop if they cannot secure these liberties. . . . We recognize that a national revolution will profit not only the bourgeoisie but also the proletariat. As a matter of fact, we should unite all the revolutionary parties, organize a joint battle line with the nationalists in order to realize our object of overthrowing the feudal militarist party and imperialistic oppression and to establish a real democratic independent nation. We should summon all the workers and peasants to join the struggle under our banner. We should tell them this struggle, though it will not completely release them from their miseries, is the first step toward aiding the workers and peasants and leads to the road where their rights may be established.["] The reason for the change in policy and the decision to present a joint battle line with the nationalists is to be found in the economic and political conditions of China. In other words, the community [communists?] began to recognize the process of evolution in history. Historical changes which take hundreds of years to accomplish could not be shortened to a few years in China. Besides the oppression of the foreign imperialistic invasion there is the oppression of the domestic military party. In every civil war, behind the party were the foreign imperialists who directed its movements and encouraged it in action. To do away with both these dire influences it was necessary to join the Nationalists to bring about a revolution. What is believed is that no social revolution can occur before the present government is overthrown. "Every bit of evidence", proclaims the manifesto[2] of 1922, "proves that what gives the Chinese people (whether he is bourgeois, worker or peasant) the greatest misery is the force of capitalistic imperialism, and of militaristic and bureaucratic feudalism. Liberty may be secured, when the revolution succeeds. We, the proletariat, observe the existing Chinese political and economic conditions, advocate that we the proletariat and the poor peasants should assist the revolutionary movement. We believe that during the struggle, there is only one way to make the revolution come about rapidly—that is the cooperation of proletarian revolutionary forces and national revolutionary forces."

(2) What do the communists demand?

---

[1] Appendix 4, p. 120 here has "nationalist" instead of "democrat."
[2] Appendix 3, Section 2 (3), p. 115.   The quotation is inexact.

The Communist Movement in China

Because the communists in the first conference adopted the non-compromise policy, they had no definite demands. What they wanted was an immediate social revolution, but as they dropped their isolated attitude, they limited their demands as follows. Considered from the point of view of keen observation of economic conditions their demands might be called progressive, and, on the contrary, because they abandoned the standard of "non-political trading" they might be regarded as regressive. What they demanded most earnestly in cooperation with the national revolutionists is as follows:[1]

1. To eliminate the civil wars, overthrow the militarist party, and lay the foundations for national peace.
2. To overthrow the oppression of international imperialism in order to reach the complete independence of the Chinese nation.
3. To unite China Proper (including Manchuria) as the real Republic of China.
4. To recognize the autonomy of Mongolia, Tibet and Turkestan as autonomous states.
5. With a free federation, to reunite China Proper, Mongolia, Tibet and Turkestan and to establish them as the United States of China, a Republic.
6. To demand the unrestricted suffrage of the workers and peasants without discrimination as to sex in the national, provincial, district, municipal and various assemblies, and absolute freedom of speech, press, meeting, assembly and strike.
7. To enact laws profitable to the workers, peasants, and women:
    A. To better the treatment of workers by
        a. Abolishing the foreman system
        b. Inaugurating the eight hour day
        c. Establishing workers' hospitals and sanitary equipment in the factories
        d. Providing for factory insurance
        e. Protecting women workers and child labor
        f. Reducing unemployment
    B. To abolish the burdensome poll tax on water transportation, and to provide for the taxation of land in the whole nation—cities and villages.
    C. To abolish the Likin tax and the extra tax, and to enforce the progressive income tax.
    D. To enact laws for the restriction of the land rent.
    E. To abolish the laws which restrict women's rights, and see that women should enjoy equal political, economic and educational rights.
    F. To reform the educational system, to provide for universal education.

Among those demands the most striking is the recognition of the inde-

---
[1] The seven points are from Appendix 3, Section 4 (2), pp. 115-16. There are minor differences.

pendence and autonomy of Mongolia, Tibet and Turkestan. The militarist class in China wished to make military units of these countries which would further uphold the feudal state, but of course the communists were violently opposed to this. "But there are some differences between life in China and in Mongolia, Tibet and Turkestan", says the manifesto,[1] "which are not only the dwelling places occupied by certain races for long periods of time but are fundamentally different in economic aspects from China proper. China proper has developed from the stage of petty agricultural handicrafts to the first period of the capitalistic productive system, while Mongolia, Tibet and Turkestan remain in the pastoral stage. If these different races with their different economic phases can be compulsorily united under the military control of those who cannot even unite China as it now exists, the result is only to expand the domain of this military control and to interrupt the progress of those people toward self-determination and autonomy, and with little profit to China Proper." What they demanded was first to make Mongolia, Tibet and Turkestan autonomous, each in its proper economic setting and thus to reunite them as part of the China Federal Republic.

(3) How the Communists act in the parliament?

One of the important features of the second conference was the reversal of opinion with regard to membership of communists in such a governing body as a parliament. The communists desired their members to seek seats in parliament so that from this position they could commence propaganda among the bourgeoisie.

"The Chinese Communist Party", they urged[2], "is the first to struggle for the benefit of the Chinese proletariat and poor peasant masses. It should rush into parliament which is menaced by the feudal militariat and which cries loudly to abolish the political evils established by the militarist party assisted and bribed by the international imperialists.["] At the same time it should in the asemblies fight for benefits to be secured for the peasants and fight[3] the young bourgeoisie who would oppress the laboring classes.

(4) On what principles do the communists plan to lead the labor movement?

In the second conference they laid stress upon concentration, enlargement, and proper direction of the labor movement which they regarded as their fundamental duty. They recognized that the labor movement in China had only developed from the first grade and had hardly more than shaken off the bondage of old guild and handicraft unions. The movement had no universal nature and was but sporadic in its action. To discipline the labor

---

[1] Appendix 3, Section 2 (1), p. 113.
[2] Quoted from Appendix 4, Decision (5), 4, p. 122. Ch'en's quotation does not jibe with his translation. The two passages taken together suggest that "the Communist Party should cry loudly to abolish political evils" instead of "parliament . . . which cries loudly . . ."
[3] The passage in Appendix 5 does not specify a fight against the young bourgeois. p. 122.

unions was an important thing and the principles they adopted may be summarized as follows:[1]

1. The Chinese Communist Party decided to concentrate its efforts upon influencing such possible members of the labor unions as railway workers, seamen, metal workers, textile workers, etc.

2. The labor union is the organ for protecting the laborers' interest. They want the laborer to enjoy the products of his labor.

3. Labor unions should make clear and recognize that there can be no similarity of interest between employer and employee.

4. The labor unions should endeavor to improve the condition of the workers.

5. Labor legislation forceful enough to impress both employer and the political governing bodies should be drafted.

6. Labor unions should struggle for national independence, citizens' rights and liberties, and occupy an independent and important position in the joint battle line with other revolutionists, but it is important for the proletariat to lead themselves.

7. In order to extend the labor unions the communists must not act singly but should aid all classes of the downtrodden.

8. There are two important platforms for the labor union to establish: one is the power of collective bargaining, and the other is the recognition that the "same wages should be paid for the same labor". "Equal wages for equal labor" does not mean to reduce the higher wages to equal the lower, but to raise the lower to equal the higher.

9. The nature of the labor union is very different from that of the guild. No employers are allowed to become members. All wage-earners, however, are persuaded to join, and in the union no sex, age, religion, position, race, nationality, political opinion, or lack of training is discriminated against.

10. The labor union is a fighting union, and not only an organ to secure benefits. Its principal activity is to struggle with the capitalist and the oppressive government.

11. Every union must have a school in which to educate its members and to develop the class consciousness of the workers.

12. The structure of each labor union must be rapidly made into a firmly united, centralized and disciplined industrial union.

13. In the labor union the first step in organization is the factory commitee which should be a group of wage earners dependent upon a union.

14. The real labor union should be upheld by class unanimity of opinion and systematic discipline. To unite the whole working class, there must be no friction between workers in any particular union, and no conflict between unions throughout the whole nation.

These are the principles adopted in the second conference. Now we come

---

[1] What follows is an abbreviation of Appendix 4, Decision (6) 1-19. However, much of the force of the Decisions has been lost in condensation.

to observe the relation of the communist party and the labor unions. The Communist Party is the army of all class conscious elements, the herald of the proletariat,—has a definite platform and its object is to overthrow the bourgeoisie and the capitalists. In its struggle to benefit the workers, the Communist Party prepared to co-operate with the Nationalists, the anarchists, even Christians at any time, but these must understand that the communist party is the political party of the laborer.

Finally, the communists point out that in every country there is a unified association of labor unions struggling with world capitalism. The unified association of the world revolutionary labor unions is the Red International Labor League. It is planned to organize the labor unions of China under the banner of the International Labor Union.

(5) How are the communists connected with the young men and women movements?[1]

Two more important decisions in this conference were connected with the young men and women movements.

In connection with the young men movement, they recognized the importance of the Chinese Young Socialist Group, and decided to co-operate with that group. What does this mean? With the progress of machine productivity, the labor of the young and weak has become necessary. In many an enterprise the young labor army have become as important an appendage of the machines as the adult workers, and the treatment of these young laborers by the capitalists is generally more cruel than that of adults. Many thousands of the youth of the oppressed classes are exploited by the bourgeoisie for financial gain and are then driven to uphold their very oppressions in every civil war or war of aggression.

The economic order of the world has been destroyed by imperialism. The bourgeoisie are now imitating the imperialists in exploiting their own workers, and the weak nations in order to restore the economic condition prior to 1914. In opposing these measures the young worker would be the first to fall. In China, the oppression of the foreign imperialists externally and of the feudal militarists internally determines the stand to be taken by the young communists. Any place where young men are exploited is the place for young communists to be active. The Chinese young men movement should not only struggle for economic and cultural benefit for young workers, should not only organize them into a proletarian army under the dictatorship of communism and the Young Men's International, but should gather in all the revolutionary forces for the Nationalists' joint batle line, and lead them to struggle to overthrow the imperialistic forces of feudalism. "Go among the labor masses" is the slogan of the Young Communist International, which Chinese Young Communists should try to follow.

Now we come to discuss the decision concerning the women movement. The principles of equality and liberty, they say, for centuries have been only

---

[1] The following is based upon Appendix 4, Decisions (7) and (8).

a decorative phrase in the civilized countries of capitalism. Under a system where economic conditions are unequal, how can the women secure equality and liberty? They only become the cheaper productive slaves used by the capitalists to control the labor market. Besides that they have to bear the burden of motherhood and preserving the family under the capitalistic social organization. Since the entrance of international capitalism into China, the proletarian women have degraded their position to that of wage-slaves, working more than twelve hours a day for cheaper wages and being treated inhumanly. In the existing order, the proletarian woman are already tortured in the cruelest way. There are still many who formerly did not belong to the laboring class who are now driven to labor by economic conditions, and still more, women in China are imprisoned in the bondage of feudal rites and live a life only comparable to that of prostitutes. As to the economic, political and educational rights, it is the common condition of all classes of women in the whole country to be deprived of them. Therefore the demands of the Chinese Communist Party at the time being for women are (1) to help women to secure the rights of universal franchise and political rights and liberty; (2) to protect women and children in industry; (3) to overthrow all the bondage of old social rites and traditions.

The reader may perhaps recall that an International Conference of Revolutionists was summoned to Moscow at the end of 1921. The changes in policy made by the Chinese Communist Party is [are] no doubt due to that conference. The Chinese Communists not only allied themselves with the Nationalists, but led the workers, young men and women, to join the joint battle line with the Nationalist Party. We have made clear why the Chinese communists changed their "no political trading" policy. What the Nationalist Party is, and what program they adopt, will be discussed in the following chapter.

CHAPTER V

The New Program of the Nationalist Party and Its Recent Tendency

While many foreign newspaper writers regard Dr. Sun Yat-sen, the head of the nationalists, as a socialist, I consider him a democrat. In order to find out what relation there is between the nationalists and the communists, it is worth while to study the book written by Dr. Sun in 1922 called "The International Development of China".

As soon as an armistice was declared in the recent World War, he took up his pen to write this book and tried to make a new program for China. His scheme may be briefly summarized as follows:

1. The development of a communication system
    A. 100,000 miles of railways
    B. 100,000 miles of macadam road
    C. Improvement of existing canals
        (a) Hangchow-Tientsin Canals
        (b) Sikiang-Yangtze Canals
    D. Construction of new canals
        (a) Liaoho-Sunghwakiang Canal
        (b) Others to be projected
    E. Conservation of waterways
        (a) To regulate the embankments and channel of the Yangtze River from Hangkow to the sea thus facilitating ocean-going ships to reach that port at all seasons
        (b) To regulate the Hwangho embankments and channel to prevent floods.
        (c) To regulate the Sikiang (river)
        (d) To regulate the Kwaiho (river)
        (e) To regulate various other rivers
        (f) The construction of more telegraph lines and telephone and wireless systems all over the country.
2. The Development of commercial harbors
    A. Three large ocean ports with a future capacity equalling New York Harbor to be constructed in North, Central and South China.
    B. Various small commercial and fishing harbors to be constructed along the coast.
    C. Commercial docks to be constructed along all navigable rivers.

3. Modern cities with public utilities to be constructed in all railway centers, termini and alongside harbors.
4. Water power development.
5. Iron and steel works and cement works on the largest scale in order to supply the above needs.
6. Mineral development.
7. Agricultural development.
8. Irrigation work on a large scale in Mongolia and Sinkiang.
9. Reforestation in Manchuria, Mongolia, Sinkiang, Kokonor, and Tibet.

In entering upon the development scheme, he calls the attention to four main points:

(1) The most remunerative field must be selected in order to attract foreign capital.
(2) The most urgent needs of the nation must be met.
(3) The lines of least resistance must be followed.
(4) The most suitable positions must be chosen.

Such a scheme, Dr. Sun believes, would help not only China, but the world. "China," he says, "a country possessing a territory of 4,289,000 square miles, a population of 400,000,000 people, and the richest mineral and agricultural resources in the world, is now a prey of militaristic and capitalistic powers . . . a greater bone of contention than the Balkan Peninsula. Unless the Chinese question can be settled peacefully, another world war will threaten, one more terrible than the last will be inevitable. In order to solve the Chinese question, I suggest that the vast resources of China be developed internationally under a socialistic scheme, for the good of the world in general and the Chinese people in particular. It is my hope that as a result of this, the present spheres of influence can be abolished; the international capitalistic competition can be got rid of, and last, but not least, the class struggle between capital and labor can be avoided." What President Wilson has proposed is to end military wars in the future through the intervention of the League of Nations, and what is also proposed is to root out the great cause of future war by ending the trade war with cooperation and mutual help in the development of China.

How can this program be worked out? Dr. Sun, with his warm heart, welcomes foreign capital. "Fortunately," he concludes, "however, soon after the preliminary part of my program has been sent out to the different governments at the Peace Conference, a new consortium was formed in Paris for the purpose of assisting China in developing her natural resources. This was initiated by the American government. Thus we need not fear the lack of capital to start work in our industrial development." What he hopes to do is to have all the great industries in China owned by Chinese people, and he claims "in my international development scheme, I intend to make all the national industries of China into a Great Trust owned by the Chinese people, and financed with internal capital for mutual benefit."

In this international development scheme, he ventures to present a practical solution for three great world problems which are international war, commercial war and class war.

To end the international war he points out the sad fate of that aggressive Germany who entirely lost her capital and interest, plus something more, while victorious France gained practically nothing. Since China is now awake, the next aggression from Japan will surely be met by a resolute resistance from the Chinese people. He also states that by cooperation, the Powers can secure more benefits and advantages than by struggle. The Chinese people, who desire to organize China for peace, will welcome heartily this New Consortium provided it will carry out the principles which are outlined in Dr. Sun's plans. Thus, cooperation of various nations can be secured and the military struggle for individual and national gain will cease forever.

In his argument advocating the end of commercial war or competition, Dr. Sun says that the result of this war is no less harmful and cruel to the vanquished foes than an armed conflict. The Adam Smith school thought that competition was a beneficent factor in a sound economic system, but modern economists discover that it is wasteful and ruinous. As a matter of fact modern economic tendencies work in a contrary direction, that is, towards concentration instead of competition. Private trusts raise the price of articles as high as possible, and the public is oppressed. The proper remedy is to have production plants owned by all the people of the country. If the industries of China be made a great trust owned by the people thus once for all commercial war will be done away with in the largest market of the world.

How to end the class war? Dr. Sun thinks it is better not to follow the old path of western civilization. The goal of modern civilization is not private profit but public profit, and the shortest route to it is not competition but cooperation. In his program, he proposes that the profit of this industrial development should go first to pay the interest and principal of foreign capital invested in it; secondly, to give high wages to labor; and thirdly, to improve or extend the machinery of production. Besides these provisions the rest of the profit should go to the public in the form of reduced prices in all commodities and public services. In a nutshell, it is his idea to make capitalism create socialism in China so that these two economic forces of human evolution will work side by side for future civilization.

What is described above is the new program of Dr. Sun, and in a word his most recent plan is to try to develop China so that she may assume the rank of a western power. For further exposition of the ideas of the Nationalists, it is well to study the ideas of Dr. Sun. During the last twenty years Dr. Sun has advocated three principles: the principle of Nationality, the principle of People's Rights, and the principle of Common Welfare. In order to uphold the principle of nationality, he overthrows the Manchurian government and restores the nationality of China proper. To uphold the principle of people's rights, he founds the Republic of China, in order to secure the freedom of the people. As to the principle of common welfare, he explains that it is to be found under socialism rather than capitalism. In his memoir, he says, "Since I escaped the iron claw of the Chinese legation in London, I plan to stay in Europe to investigate politics and customs. During the two years I have been here I have added much to my knowledge, and begin to understand what peoples' rights really mean. Europe as at present constituted does not make the people really free, so pioneers in social reform are struggling to introduce a social revolution. If China will adopt the methods toward social reform which I advocate, the greatest happiness of the greatest number will be assured.["] Though we do not believe that Dr. Sun's method is exactly socialism, it is unquestionably possible for it to reach the goal of state-socialism. Although Dr. Sun has interpreted his principles as socialism, the communist party regards him as a nationalist rather than socialist. The communists enter his party only from the point of view of nationalism and not of socialism. In the decision of the second conference is found the statement[1] that "China is a republic in name but controlled by the feudal militarist's power in fact; and externally it is a semi-independent nation controlled by international imperialistic powers. Under such economic and political conditions, and under such internal and external two-fold pressure, the proletariat, because there is no other way to secure freedom, must fight for it, that is, join the national revolutionary movement. We ought to know that this joining does not mean that we surrender to the nationalists who only represent the bourgeoisie, to be their vassals, and also by no means does it follow that the victory of nationalism will completely emancipate the proletariat; but it is a fact that temporary union with the nationalists is necessary for us to overthrow the pressure of our enemies—the feudal militarists internally and the international imperialists externally; the proletariat have no other way of securing the freedom. . . . The nationalist party is not the party that represents the proletariat and struggles for the proletariat."

To join the joint battle line with the nationalists is the proposal suggested by the central executive committee, approved and decided upon by the second conference of the national representatives. The program states:[2] "The Nationalist Party and the Young Socialist Group are called upon to open a representative conference in a suitable place to discuss the best methods of summoning the other revolutionary parties and working out this program." When they opened the conference and how the program was carried out is unknown to anyone, but in July 1922, a proclamation was issued by the communist central committee asking all its members to enter the Nationalist Party. This proclamation was voluntary rather than compulsory in nature. The communist party simultaneously issued a manifesto to announce the reason and necessity for cooperation with the nationalist party, and the communist magazine, "Forward", began propaganda for nationalism.

So far as we know, these ideas had never been carefully explained before. Since the communists have joined the nationalists, the Nationalist Party has

---
[1] From Appendix 4, Decisions, (3) paragraph 3, with slight discrepancies.
[2] From Appendix 4, Decisions, (3) A.

amended its program and has written a detailed explanation of the three great principles which Dr. Sun advocates. The three principles are given briefly as follows:

(A) The three principles for the People.

1. The Principle of Nationality. Upon the foundation of existing nationality, to construct a nation of Pan-Chinese, to realize a nationalistic country.
2. The Principle of Peoples' Rights. To realize peoples' rights, and political and sex equality, and to secure the following rights for the people:
    a. the right of the ballot. The members of various assemblies and local officials are elected by people in the form of direct and universal franchise.
    b. the right of initiative. When the local legislative body can not enact or amend a certain law petitioned by the people, the people may legally assemble or vote for the initiative.
    c. the right of referendum. When the bill voted or vetoed by the local legislative body is recognized as unsuitable, the people may legally assemble to vote again upon it.
    d. the right of dismissal. When the members of various assemblies or local officials recognize an office-holder as unfaithful to his duties, the people may legally assemble to dismiss him by vote.
3. The Principle of Common Welfare.
To avoid the inequality between capital and labor, to harmonize the inequality of society, the first step in the policy to develop the whole resources of the people is as follows:
    a. The establishment of National Industries. Industries belonging to the whole people should be under the management and control of the government.
    b. Equalization of rights to the land. A land law, a law concerning distribution of the land, and for taxing the price of land should be enacted in order to equalize the right to the land.
    c. Protection of Labor. A law to protect and to improve the welfare of the workers and peasants should be enacted.

(B) Five Constitutional Rights.

1. The Right of the legislative bodies to enact various laws and supervise finance.
2. The Right of the Judiciary to conduct trials of various actions.
3. The Right of the Executive to administer.
4. The Right to inspect the officials and the members of various assembles.

5. The Right to examine the citizens for civil service and to decide upon fitness to hold office.
Dr. Sun is responsible for the last two rights.

Since 1911 Dr. Sun has changed his attitude with regard to the extension of nationalism. At first he confined it to China proper, but now he wishes to admit Manchuria, Mongolia, Tibet and Turkestan to the Chinese Republic. The Nationalist Party simultaneously organized two new committees or departments to take charge of the affairs of workers, peasants, and women. The function of the committee of peasants and workers is to investigate the conditions of foreign peasants and workers and to search for suggestions to improve the condition of Chinese peasants and workers. The function of the committee is to investigate the conditions of foreign and domestic women, and to discover how to help women in China.

The reform program is the program of the Nationalists after cooperation with the communists. Surely Dr. Sun desires to push China into what he calls socialism, but it is very different from the principles the communists adopted. In the last two years, it has been rumoured that Dr. Sun tends toward Red Organization and an alliance with Russia, which is only a suspicion caused by jealousy and prejudice in the diplomatic circle and among the capitalists in China. So far as I know Dr. Sun has never had a desire to make China red. As a matter of fact, nationalism is nationalism, and communism is communism, there is no chance for them to be intermingled. The reason why the communists desire to cooperate with the nationalists is because nationalism can perhaps improve the proletariat. Dr. Sun is not a Socialist and does not advocate reform through "red" measures.

The cooperation of those parties will surely be an important and a great change worthy of the future historian. Now those two parties are struggling in South China as well as in the North. Whether their program will be worked out will depend upon the persistence and patience of the two. As to the result no one can forecast what will happen, and we have to wait for time to answer.

CHAPTER VI

The Third Conference of the Chinese Communist Party and Conclusion

There may arise the question how long and how far can the communists co-operate with the nationalists. Though they ally themselves temporarily, the foundations of the two parties were originally distinct. The nationalists represent the bourgeoisie while the communists the proletariat. The latter denies the right to private ownership, the former recognizes it. The latter resists international capitalism, the former accepts it. The latter recognizes the independence of Mongolia, Tibet and Turkestan, the former refuses to recognize such independence. A characteristic of the revolution advocated by the latter is that it should be international, and the revolution of the former is national only.

In July, 1923, the third conference of the Chinese Communist Party was held in Canton where Dr. Sun's government is situated. This conference made few changes in its decisions and policies as compared with the first conference, but it issued a manifesto not very satisfactory to the nationalists, and pointed out some steps the nationalist party had taken. Considering the political and economic features of the world and of China, considering the misery and the demands of the Chinese social classes, they still insisted that a national revolution was necessary, but they were dissatisfied with the military action, and had only contempt for the mass propaganda of the Nationalist Party.

"The Nationalist Party of China," the manifesto runs, "should be the central force of the national revolution, and should lead the national revolution; but unfortunately the Nationalists have two wrong ideas, e.g. (1) they hope that the Powers will help the Chinese in a national revolution, which not only would cause the nationalists to lose leadership in the revolution but make the people depend upon a foreign power, and would discourage the spirit of independence and self-confidence in the people, (2) they concentrate their efforts only upon military action, without paying any attention to the need for propaganda among the people. For these two reasons the Nationalists lose their political leadership, and we believe that the national revolutionists because of their lack of the sympathy with the people will never succeed with only military action.

"We still hope that all of the social revolutionary elements will join the nationalists in order that a national revolution may come about rapidly; at the same time we also hope that the nationalists will dare to abandon their two old ideas of dependence upon the Powers, and concentration of their efforts upon military action. We hope they will pay more attention to political propaganda among the masses in order to establish real central forces of social welfare and real leadership for the national revolution." But when I began to write this thesis, a telegram printed by a Chinese newspaper in San Francisco stated that the propaganda of the communists was prohibited by the Canton government. No detailed report has since been received but if this be true, the co-operation of these two parties will be stopped and the gulf between them will perhaps become wider afterwards.

In fact, the communists explain that the reason they ally themselves with the nationalists is only for the temporary benefit to be gained; they will split in the long run. The communists always warn the workers that they should not only participate in the national revolutionary battle line on the one hand, but should struggle to improve their own position on the other; that the reason for joining the nationalists' battle line is that the working class may secure political power and that the alignment with the nationalists is only a matter of policy. During the struggle the proletariat ought to join and assist the nationalists, but by no means surrender or become mere appendages, because the nationalist party is not the party that represents the proletariat and struggles for the proletariat. They should, on the contrary, assemble the proletariat . . . under the banner of the Chinese Communist Party, and agitate the movement for their own class independently. The proletariat should not forget their own independent organization during the struggle.

As far as the political struggle is concerned they must join the nationalists, but in the labor movement, they must keep their independent attitude. The second conference decided that "the communists, when active in the labor unions organized by nationalists, anarchists or Christians, should not be permitted to direct the workers to leave the organized unions arbitrarily. Our tactics are to encourage a gradual assumption of power in these unions and thus to be able to overthrow the leadership of the Nationalists, Anarchists or Christians."

That these two parties will eventually split is very clear to the communists. This is pointed out in the following statement, "After the success of the revolution the nationalists will tend naturally toward oppression of the proletariat by the very political powers they have seized from the feudalists. At the same time the strength of the proletariat will be determined by the ability to organize and to fight which the proletariat can cultivate during the revolutionary period." The split in their friendship will come sooner or later, but it is too early to say that it has begun now. When the nationalists succeed they will break with the communists. It is rash to forecast a sudden change. Time alone will tell us. This will probably suffice for a description of the communist movement in China. How far they can succeed depends upon the poignancy of the suffering inflicted upon China by the imperialists. The object of Europe in her relations with China is primarily, it seems to me, not to establish friendly relations, but to use China for selfish purposes of gain by fair means or foul, the motives of "pirates rather than peaceably disposed men." We do not repeat the enlightened military intrusion of the imperialists to China, but speak of the recent peaceful conferences, we can hardly point out which is the just one for the weak. It is no wonder that Mr. Hughes, the Secretary of State of the United States, said, "The best of diplomatic instruments, the conference, has no magical potency to dispose of the strongly held national convictions."

In China, every conference seems a new source of trouble. The more the Great Powers meet, the more her misery increases. The Paris Conference of 1919 was no doubt a reactionary conference just like the Vienna Conference directed by Metternich. China was arbitrarily disposed of as if she were a defeated enemy. Shantung was granted as a donation to Japan, and the Japanese twenty-one demands were quietly recognized by the Powers. The small states each lifted a piping treble of protest, but no one paid any attention. The world has eagerly promised everything in November! The world was to be made over; nations were to be just and generous; war was to be abolished! But in January what a change! A new militarism and a new system of armed alliances were made worse than the old. In fact, as the Chinese communists well said, the Paris Conference was a booty-apportioning conference, in which the German colonies were handed about and the spheres of influence in Near and Far East were newly realigned.

Next came the Washington Conference, in which Mr. Hughes advocated six policies, namely: (1) the Open Door, (2) the maintenance of China as an integral whole, (3) co-operation with other powers in the declaration of common principles, (4) co-operation with other powers by conference and consultation in the interests of peace, (5) the limitation of naval armament, and (6) the limitation of fortifications and naval bases. But in what way do all these policies particularly aid China? However successful the conference may have been in other respects, its solution of the Chinese problem was far from satisfactory. Three out of the six leased territories are still to be retained indefinitely by Great Britain and Japan, even the remaining four which were to be returned to China are still under consideration, the deliberations prolonged from month to month and a special compensation and redemption of other privileges demanded. The abolition of consular jurisdiction is to take effect only when an international commission of jurists appointed for the special purpose shall report in its favor. The alien post offices are still to stay in the leased territories and foreign concessions after January 1923, although the other alien postal establishments shall be withdrawn from Chinese territory after that date. The tariff restriction is still fastened on China and the rate is increased to five per cent ad valorem, with two and one half percent surtax if the Likin or the inter-provincial transit tax is abolished as well as five percent surtax on luxuries.

The observations of the Chinese communists may be true or not, but their manifesto says,[1] "that after the Great War, the United States, because of exclusion from the European market, overproduction, and an economic crisis, planned to develop the Far East as her only measure of relief. But on the one hand, opposition from Japan was serious, and on the other hand, there was an important problem namely—would Great Britain continue the alliance with Japan to monopolize the Far East privileges or ally with the United States to effect a simultaneous invasion of these markets? The Washington Conference was called to solve these difficulties. This conference was to apportion anew the Far East markets, and to conciliate the two inevitably conflicting policies of Japan and America, and of Great Britain and America. The Far East problem in the eyes of Great Britain was only one of her many colonial problems, so extreme measures to enforce her will might be postponed. But in Japan, as well as in America, the Far East was the only market they could develop, so a conflict of interests was imminent, and war might have broken out in the near future. How could the Washington Conference help? Only by butchering China once more, offering the products of the laboring masses of the Far East—especially China—as food for the diplomats' and bankers' dinner table in Washington to satisfy their greedy appetites.

"The reason why the Washington conference advocated the reduction or limitation of armament was to deceive the laboring classes who suffered under the heavy burden of armament. Armament is the cornerstone of the capitalistic nations. They not only need armament to help invade the weak nations, but to keep down their own laboring classes who might protest against these invasions. So the reduction of armament is absolutely impossible in a capitalistic nation. During the debate, the arguments concerning the ratio of principal battleship tonnage, and the maintenance of air and land armament revealed imperialistic plots, preparation for the next world war, and plans to oppress the labor classes.

"The principal problem in the Washington Conference—the problem of China—was made the special charge of the United States. The result was that they recognized the Japanese exploitation of Manchuria, Mongolia and East Siberia, and the establishment of China under joint control of the Powers, the "Open Door Policy". The reason why the United States adopted the old policy of Mr. John Hay is because they hoped to break the superior force of Japan and Britain with such a policy, and so the United States might assume control of Chinese economic life. The adoption of the Open Door Policy is obviously the first successful step in American commercial invasion. Though the Anglo-Japanese Alliance which had controlled China for many years was abolished, the newly established Quadruple Alliance (Britain, the United States, France, and Japan) is stronger. The New Consortium led by the United States was established by the conference, and this enables the peasantry of China to become tributary workers in the international trust. Thereafter the poor Chinese peasants have to pay taxes and rents to the

---

[1] From Appendix 3, pp 109-10, but not an entirely accurate quotation.

foreign bankers, and the industries become the private property of the foreign banks.

"The Washington Conference introduces a new feature in international affairs which substitutes for the competitive exploitation of imperialist co-operative exploitation; this will completely overthrow Chinese economic independence and will compel 400,000,000 Chinese people to enter into slavery under the new international trust. This is death to China. It is necessary for us to rise up in revolt."

Mr. Ray Standard Baker is an American whose criticism is very keen. In "The Versailles Treaty and After", he says, "If America truly wants peace and good order in the world, and is willing to make the sacrifices and take the necessary chances, she can have it. She is great and powerful enough to do nearly what she will. But she is divided in her own soul: she wants good things, but does not want them passionately enough. She is governed—exactly like Europe—by her immediate fears, her imemdiate selfish interests; she does not look into the future; she is neither truly idealistic nor truly practical."

"The flesh of the weak is the dinner of the strong", as the old Chinese proverb says. Though the imperialists cry out against war in general, they are never averse to increasing armament in the interest of exploitation. Forms of the wars may be changed but their characteristics remain the same. "Meanwhile the economic ruin of China still proceeds. Since 1905 the competition between the imperialist states and their groups of financiers has been modified. The Russo-Japanese War and other events showed clearly that this competition to exploit China, if carried to its logical conclusion, not only led to expensive wars between the competitors, but reduced the financial profits which might be squeezed out of the Chinese people. International competition now gives way to a curious form of international co-operation. The chief financial interests of Britain, France, America and Japan join together in a consortium. Under this system the several financial groups are still backed by their governments, but elaborate arrangements are made for sharing the loans made to and the economic concessions granted by China. This, however, does not mean that any real attempt is made to safeguard Chinese rights or interests, for the object of the consortium is the financial interests of the consortium. The modern economic form of slavery may be less distressing to the consciences of sentimental people, but it is just as effective as the old. It is very interesting in this regard to quote Chief Justice Marshall: "No principle is more universally acknowledged than the perfect equality of nations. . . . It results from this equality that no one can rightfully impose a rule upon another." His idea is all right, but it is a pity that it is only right for the powers, not for China.

Communism is essentially a product of the nineteenth century, and is especially the last resort of miserable people. How far the Chinese communists succeed depends upon how miserably they suffer from capitalism and imperialism. I should like to end this chapter with a quotation from the

Communist manifesto:[1] "Three hundred millions of Chinese peasants are the important factors of our revolutionary movement. The peasants are in misery for several reasons—lack of land, density of population, prevalence of calamity, civil war and banditry, extra-taxes imposed by militarists, pressure of foreign commodities and the increasing cost of living. . . . If these poor peasants hope to escape from this miserable environment, there is only one way for them—that is revolution. And it is to be believed that the Chinese revolution will immediately succeed, when the majority of the peasants ally with the workers."

---

[1] From Appendix 3, p. 114, but not exact.

Appendix 1

The First Program of the Communist Party of China 1921

1. Our Party adopts the name "The Communist Party of China" (C.P.C.).
2. The programs of our Party are as follows:
   A. With the revolutionary army of the proletariat to overthrow the capitalistic classes, to reconstruct the nation from the labor class, until class distinctions are eliminated.
   B. To adopt the dictatorship of the proletariat in order to complete the end of class struggle—abolishing the classes.
   C. To overthrow the private ownership of capital, to confiscate all the productive means, such as machines, land, buildings, semi-manufactured products, etc., and to entrust them to social ownership.
   D. To unite with the Third international.
3. Our Party, with the adoption of the Soviet form, organizes the industrial and agricultural laborers and soldiers, preaches communism, and recognizes the social revolution as our chief policy; absolutely cuts off all relations with the yellow intellectual class, and other such parties.
4. No discrimination as to sex or nationality is allowed in the membership; anyone who accepts the programs and policies of our Party and who promises loyalty to our Party after introduction by one of our members, can be our comrade, but before he enters our Party, he shall sever relation with any party or group which opposes our program.
5. The procedure for introducing a member is this: the candidate should be suggested to the local soviet for investigation; the time for investigation is at most limited to two months. After investigation, through the consent of the majority of the members, the membership of the new applicant is recognized. If in that locality an Executive Committee has been established, this membership should be approved by that committee.
6. Until the time for disclosure is ripe the doctrines of the party and even membership in it must be kept secret.
7. In any locality which has as many as five members, a local soviet can be organized.
8. The member of a soviet, through a formal introduction from his local secretary can transfer to another local soviet.
9. In any local soviet, numbering less than ten members, only one secretary is appointed to manage affairs; if the soviet has over ten members, a treasurer, an organizer, and a propagandist should be appointed; if the

soviet has over thirty members, an executive committee should be organized. The rules of such a committee will be stipulated hereafter.
10. In various localities, when the membership increases, the organizations of laborers, peasants, soldiers, and students should be utilized for the external activity according to occupations, but such organizations should be under the direction of the local executive committee.
12.[1] The finances, publications and the policies of any local soviet shall be supervised and directed by the Central Executive Committee.
13. When the members exceed five hundred or when more than five local executive committees have been established in the whole country, a convenient place should be chosen in which to organize the Executive Committee including ten members elected by the national representative conference. When the above-mentioned conditions are not carried out, a Provisional Central Executive Committee should be organized to meet the necessity. The detailed regulations of the Central Executive Committee will be stipulated thereafter.
14. The members, unless they are under the pressure of existing law or have obtained consent from the party, can not be government officials or members of parliament, but soldiers, policemen and civil service employees are not held to this restriction. (This article provoked a bitter discussion, and at last it was postponed for the second conference to decide in 1922.)
15. This program can be amended when a bill concerning such amendment is passed by two-thirds of the representatives of the National Representative Conference.

[1] There is no 11. in Ch'en's text. It may have dropped out when he typed a new page, or he may have misnumbered after 10.

Appendix 2

The First Decision as to the Object of the Communist Party of China 1921

(1) Labor Organization

To form industrial unions is the chief aim of our party. In any locality where there is more than one kind of industry an industrial union shall be organized; if there is no great industry in a certain locality but only one or two factories, a factory-union can be organized suitable to conditions in that locality.

The party should imbue the unions with the spirit of the class struggle. If the political struggle, fostered by various unions does not agree with our program, this party should avoid becoming the puppet of other parties.

As to the existing guilds and technical unions, this party is allowed to send members to join these organizations in order to take the first step toward reorganization.

A labor union cannot be formed unless more than two hundred members can be secured. At least two of our members should be sent to a new union to aid in organization.

(2) Propaganda

Magazines, daily publications, encyclopedia, and pamphlets must all be under the management of the Central Executive Committee or the Provisional Central Executive Committee.

Each locality can publish a union magazine, a daily and a weekly paper and pamphlets and temporary circulars according to its needs.

Whether a publication is central or local, it should be directly managed and edited by the members of the party.

Any publication of a central or local must not contain articles inconsistent with the principles, policies, and decisions of the party.

(3) Labor Supplementary Schools

As a labor supplementary school is the preparatory step in the organization of an industrial union, such schools should be formed within the units of various industries, such as the Transportation supplementary labor school, the Textile supplementary labor school, etc. No supplementary school teaching several different kinds of work is permitted, excepting in those cases where the need for such an arrangement is unanswerable.

In the supplementary school, only workers can be members of the managing board of the school to take charge of school affairs. Teachers are employed by the party, but they can attend such board meetings.

Labor supplementary schools should gradually become the centres of labor organs; otherwise they are not permitted and can be stopped or reorganized by the party according to conditions.

The most important doctrine taught should be that which can awake the consciousness of laborers and show them the need for organizing labor unions.

(4) Institution for studying labor organization

This institution should be organized by the leaders of various industries, class-conscious workers, and the comrades of the party, and should teach the proper methods of industrial organization.

The object of such an institution is to discipline the workers who carry on the practical work of the party so that special attention can be paid to such phases as organization of labor unions, help in the various other movements of the proletariat, and investigation of the conditions of the labor unions and of the proletariat.

For the purpose of increasing the ability of the members, the institution may be divided into research groups in the following subjects: history of the labor movement, the method of organizing factory laborers, Karl Marx's economic theories, the present aspects of the labor movement of various nations. The results of this research may be published in a series. (In the discussion of these problems, special attention is paid to local conditions in China.)

(5) The attitude towards the existing political parties

Towards the existing political parties, an attitude of independence, aggression and exclusion should be adopted. In the political struggle, in opposition to militarism and bureaucracy and in demanding freedom of speech, press, and assemblage, when we must declare our attitude, our party should stand up in behalf of the proletariat, and should allow no relationship with the other parties or groups.

(6) The relation between the party and the Third International

The Central Organ should make a report to the Third International every month. If necessary, a formal representative should be sent to the station in the Far East Secretariat of the Third International in Irkuchika, and deputies should be sent to the various Far East nations to further plans for union in the class struggle.

Appendix 3

The Manifesto of the Communist Party of China adopted in July 1922 by the Second Congress

1. China under the control of the International Imperialism

(1)

The development of Europe and America depends largely upon the exploitation of Africa and Asia. During the last century, capitalism, by its aggressive spirit has built the colossal figure of the bloody world capitalism. These capitalistic imperialists, beginning with competition and exploitation, and ending in war, have reduced the economic life of the world down to skeleton proportions. They are now working to restore it to a normal state of health, and when sufficiently restored, they will commence again the old tactics which brought it to its present low estate. Under this process there are 1,250,000,000 people of the colonies and oppressed nations (besides billions [millions] of proletariat in the capitalistic countries) who are tortured under the pressure of a small minority of bankers and entrepreneurs in London, Paris, New York or Tokyo. This cruel and miserable condition will be eliminated, provided that the capitalistic organization of the world be uprooted. It is worthwhile to make this point clear, because all the Chinese, not only the labor class, should know the reason why they have suffered.

It is necessary for the capitalistic nations to possess a large market in order to sell their overproduction, and to provide the necessary raw materials. The only markets they can exploit are India, China, Turkey, Morocco, Egypt, Persia, Korea, Mexico, Indo-China, Malay Strait Archipaligoes, and South and Central Africa, so that competition is to bring on war. The slaughter of 1914 to 1918 partly originated in the conflict of two different camps of capitalistic imperialism, namely Great Britain and Germany, in their raids upon the Near East market.

The effect of the World War was to slaughter millions of the labor classes, to annex the German colonies, to destroy German and Austrian economic foundations, and to transform them into British and French colonies, in a word to overturn the economic order of the world without mercy. After the war, the imperialistic nations planned to restore the economic conditions prevailing previous to 1914, and in order to remedy the capitalistic depression, plotted to compensate the losses of war by raiding the labor classes. They called several conferences in Paris, Washington, and Genoa, and under the pretext of "peace", "justice" they attempted to fool the oppressed classes, but the fact that the bitter conflict had been caused by their desire to exploit and to control the world is revealed to all.

No matter how many times the imperialists call their conferences, it is evident that they cannot bring an end to the British-French conflict except through force of arms. Though capitalists are often urged to do their best to relieve the world's economic crisis, it can by no ways be remedied by capitalism. Hoping to escape from the fire of social revolution, they try to postpone war by means of these conferences, compromising themselves, dividing their booty, and sacrificing the weak nations' profits. At the same time they also hurriedly rob the resources and labor of the colonies and weak nations; on the one hand, they can temporarily yoke their own proletariat in the harness gradually making good the war losses, and, on the other hand, they devote their efforts to the preparation of economic and military forces for the next world war.

For many years the Oriental nations have been tortured under the iron heels of the British, the Americans, the Japanese, and the French, and since the Great War, the advance of imperialism has been more pronounced. The United States holds the Philippines, pretending to be kind, but continuing her economic conquest of these islands without any mercy; Britain clutches the throat of India, suppressing the Indian independence movement, in order to maintain the existing condition under which a million of Indian laborers die under the British claws. Annam peasants slave like cattle under the French imperialistic pressure, planting rice and corn to maintain the supply for French merchants. No matter how many peasants are starving in Annam, millions of tons of rice are prepared for export by the French merchants every year; and the Japanese are mercilessly crushing Korean trade with the enormous import of Japanese goods, and compulsory export of rice, making twenty million Koreans starve.

The process by which the imperialistic Great Powers have entered China is sufficient to reveal the hidden schemes of international capitalism and imperialism. China, because she possesses unlimited fertile land, numerous raw products, and millions of cheap labor, attracts the greedy desire of capitalistic powers, and competition and exploitation.

(2)

The entrance of imperialism into China began with the aggressive acts of the British fleet in 1839, a most piratical action. The underlying cause was the determination of the English government and merchants to poison the Chinese people with opium. From the attacking of Taku by the Anglo-French alliance army in 1850 [sic] to the Boxer Rebellion against foreigners in 1901 [sic], which caused the Eight Nations alliance to occupy Peking, is a period of forty-three years during which bloody time the capitalistic nations butchered China, and it is also the most miserable and degrading period in Chinese history. The opening of the twentieth century has added a new feature in the conflict of the Great Powers with each other over the exploitation of nations inferior in power. The cause of the Russo-Japanese war was the robbery of Manchuria. The cost of this conflict was no doubt paid by Chinese flesh and blood.

During eighty years' invasion by the imperialistic powers, China, as a matter of fact, has become their joint colony. The imperialists not only occupy the broad territories, islands and protectorates and new colonies, but have robbed China of many important harbors in order to create foreign settlements; and at last have divided China into several spheres of influence in order to realize their monopolistic exploitation policy. In China one-third of the railways are owned by the foreign capitalists, others are also directly or indirectly controlled by the foreign creditors. Foreign steamers freely navigate in Chinese harbors and rivers, postal and telegraph services are closely supervised, and the tariff is dependent and controlled by the foreign imperialists—under such a regime it is not only convenient for the foreigners to import their capital, absorb raw material, but worst of all, the soul of Chinese economic life has mercilessly been clutched in the imperialistic claw. The foreign capitalists also occupy many mines, they have established factories in Shanghai and Tientsin, and drive the Chinese laborers with whips in the mines and factories as their productive slaves. At the same time the imports of foreign commodities rise like a relentless tide. Not only the cloth and paper, but the old home-made needles and nails are obliged to give way to the imported ones. The disastrous effect is the rise in the cost of living. Three hundred millions of peasants tend to become paupers, the living of ten million of handicraftsmen is jeopardized by the handsome imported manufactured commodities. Cash indemnities were demanded of China at the end of every war. The compound interest of $2,000,000,000 upon foreign loans, and the control of foreign bankers in Shanghai, Peking, Tientsin, Hankow and Canton, affected the economic life of the nation, and the people are sorely harassed. The imperialists also bribe the bureaucratic politicians, send many advisers and missionaries to China, publish newspapers, and establish schools, all of which are only contrivances to spread imperialistic propaganda. They also contrive to secure the Consular jurisdiction privilege, and station their armies, police, and fleets in the territory of China.

(3)

Since the outbreak of the Great War, as the Europeans and Americans have no time to watch the Orient, the Japanese imperialists utilize this opportunity to brush aside the German authority in Shangtung, occupy Kiaochow Bay, and with bribery and threats, oppress China with those notorious Twenty-one Demands in order to change China into a Japanese colony. Since then, the influence of Japanese imperialism has penetrated the very heart of executive, financial, military, diplomatic and political life in China; controls the economic growth of China, and freely directs the Peking government toward the realization of a colonizing policy. Of course this result satisfies the Japanese imperialists, but on the other hand, it evokes the jealousy of American imperialists, and the differences between Japanese and Americans in China become greater and greater.

At the end of the Great War came the Paris Conference which was in reality the booty-apportioning conference, in which the German colonies were given away, and the spheres of influence in Near and Far East were newly aligned. In that conference, Japan had already secured too many privileges from China, and the American imperialists could hardly agree to such a state of affairs. As the difference of opinion could not be reconciled by a satisfactory apportionment of China, the problem was set aside. But the plan of exploiting China by both Japan and the United States was very clearly expressed.

As the United States could not agree with Japan concerning their operations in China, at the Paris Conference, a New Consortium was planned—an international imperialistic trust formed so that capital might be exported by the United States and with this superior economic force the United States would reach the preferential position in exploiting China, and would assume control of Chinese economic life. But because Japan refused to agree to this plan, for she had occupied a great portion of Chinese territory as her sphere of influence, the plan of this New Consortium was for the time being unsuccessful.

Under the conflicting direction of the American and Japanese governments the present peculiar political situation of China has been brought about. The Japanese imperialists assisted the Peking government which was controlled by the An-Fu Party, the war-lord Chang Tso-lin, and the Old and

New Communicationists Clubs, because the Japanese planned the penetration of China with the Peking government as their tool. The British stand behind General Wu Pei-fu, because they want to increase their privileges and expand their influence along the Yangtse River. The United States allies itself with the newly prosperous Chinese bourgeoisie and intellectuals, because the Americans want to establish an international policy of trust.

(4)

After the Great War, the United States, because of exclusion from the European market, overproduction, and an economic crisis, planned to develop the Far East market as her only measure of relief. But, on the one hand, opposition from Japan was serious, and on the other hand, there was an important problem, namely—would Great Britain continue the alliance with Japan which monopolized the Far East privileges, or would Great Britain join with the United States to effect a simultaneous invasion of these markets. The Washington Conference was called to solve these difficulties. This conference had two objects: to apportion anew the Far East markets, and to conciliate the two inevitably conflicting policies of Japan and America, and of Great Britain and America. The Far East problem in the eyes of Great Britain was only one of her many colonial problems, so that conflict with America might be postponed. But in Japan, as well as in America, the Far East was the only market to be developed, so a conflict of interest was imminent, and war might have broken out in the near future.

How could the Washington Conference help? Only by offering up the products of the laboring masses of the Far East—especially China—as food for the diplomatists' and bankers' dinner table in Washington to satisfy their greedy appetites.

The reason why the Washington Conference advocated the reduction of armament was to deceive the laboring classes who suffered under the heavy burden of armament and who might rise up in revolt. Armament is the cornerstone of the capitalistic nations. They not only need armament to invade the weak nations, but to keep down their own laboring classes who might protest these invasions. So the reduction of armament is absolutely impossible in a capitalistic nation. During the debate, the arguments concerning the ratio of principal battleship tonnage, and the maintenance of air and land armament revealed imperialistic plots, preparation for the next world war, and plans to oppress the labor classes.

The principal problem in the Washington Conference—the problem of China—was made the special charge of the United States. The result was that they recognized the Japanese exploitation of Manchuria, Mongolia, and East Siberia, and the establishment of China under joint control of the Powers in the "Open Door Policy". The reason why the United States adopted the old policy of Mr. John Hay is because they hoped to break down the superior force of Japan and Britain with such a policy, and so that the United States might assume the control of Chinese economic life. The adoption of the

Open Door policy is obviously the first successful step of American commercial invasion. Though the Anglo-Japanese Alliance which had controlled China for many years was abolished, the newly established Quadruple Alliance (Britain, the United States, France and Japan) —is not so strong as the Anglo-Japanese Alliance but is stronger than the old competitive policy. The New Consortium led by the United States was given a more firm foothold in the conference, and this enabled the peasantry of China to become the tributary workers in the international trust. Thereafter the poor Chinese peasants have to pay taxes and rents to foreign bankers, and the industries become the private property of the foreign banks.

The Washington Conference introduces a new feature into China—it substitutes for the competitive exploitation of imperialism cooperative exploitation. This will completely overthrow Chinese economic independence and will compel 400,000,000 Chinese people to enter into slavery under the new international trust. This is death to China. It is necessary for us to rise up in revolution.

(5)

All of the facts described above show why the imperialistic powers enter China and raid Chinese workers and peasants. The imperialists are still shamelessly shouting the slogan "Equality of nations, self-determination and equality of human beings", and contrive smoothly to conceal their actions, in which the capitalistic class exploit the proletarian class, and the strong nations oppress the weak nations. But the Chinese people, through experience of oppression during ninety years, are able to understand what the "Equality and self-determination" as pronounced by the imperialists really means, and also understand that equality and self-determination cannot be realized until capitalistic imperialism has been overthrown.

So the oppressed Chinese labor masses ought to understand conditions existing throughout the world, otherwise they cannot release themselves from the misery of oppression. Recent world politics show two opposite tendencies. The first is the capitalistic and imperialistic policy of the Great Powers, who unanimously intrigue to control the proletariat and the oppressed nations of the whole world, and the second is the revolutionary movement to overthrow the international capitalistic imperialism, as exemplified in International Communists and Soviet Russia—the movement of world revolution and the movement of national revolution in the various oppressed nations. After the Great War British productivity was in a state of stagnation, the French economic life was bankrupt, the productivity of the United States was too great for wise control and the imperialists found no way to restore the economic conditions existing prior to the war. The reason they organized the League of Nations was to further the policy of mutual insurance which will respect the privileges already secured and maintain production, but a result very different from this came unexpectedly.

The Washington Conference made clear the conflicts between America and Japan, the Genoa Conference showed the lack of accord between Britain and France. Destruction due to the war has overtaken the capitalistic wall, of which the possibility of an accidental fall appears probable at any time. This strongly proves that world capitalism is near its end. Soviet Russia of the workers and peasants—the marvelous cornerstone of the world revolutionary labor mass—continuously attacks world capitalism, and its power has been strengthened through its five years' struggle. The flame of the German and Central European proletarian revolutions reaches its fiercest height. Many terrible strikes frequently occur in England, the United States, Italy, and France, all of which already shake the camp of imperialism. In Japan, the power of the revolutionary movement of the proletariat increases to some extent. Among the oppressed nations of India, Egypt, Ireland and Korea, affected by the Great War and the Russian Revolution, the independent revolutionary movement has reached the stage of organization, which frightens the imperialists and hampers their movements, tying them up hand and foot. This all shows the expansion of the revolutionary power of anti-imperialism.

These two anti-capitalistic and anti-imperialistic revolutionary forces—the proletarian revolution and the national revolution—tend to become closely allied, and this alliance will certainly push the world capitalistic skeleton into the grave dug by itself. Within recent decades, the power of anti-capitalism in China has been progressive, and will increasingly extend. But the Chinese anti-imperialistic movement should emerge into the revolutionary tide of the oppressed nations of the world and ally itself with the proletarian revolutionary class—international capitalistic imperialism. This is the only road forward for the Chinese labor mass who need to emancipate themselves from imperialistic oppression.

2. **The Existing home politics and economic aspects of the oppressed labor masses.**

(1)

On the one hand, as the imperialistic powers secure the power of controlling the economic and political privilege in China, we find politics and economic life indifferently managed by them. Because Chinese economic life is based upon semi-primeval agriculture and handicraft carried on by the family far from the period of industrial capitalization, the nation is under the management of militaristic and bureaucratic feudalism. The militarists, utilized and managed by the foreign capitalistic imperialists on the one side, plotting for their own selfish privileges on the other, break up China—the most obvious example is the occupation of Manchuria by the war lord Chang Tso-lin. From such a complicated economic and political foundation arise the difficulties and civil wars of China.

The existing political situation of China has inaugurated another new feature, which is not only advantageous to the imperialists in furthering a joint penetration policy decided upon at the Washington Conference, but prolongs the complicated state of affairs in China. In the recent civil war between Chihli and Fengtien, the British and American imperialists stood at the back of General Wu Pei-fu. They wanted to assist him to overthrow Japanese control in Peking in order to take charge of Chinese politics themselves; and on the side of Chang Tso-lin was of course the assistance of Japanese imperialists who hoped to maintain the position of the Communication Club Cabinet subsidized by Chang Tso-lin, indirectly holding the superior show of power in the Peking government. As a result of this civil war, the power of Chang Tso-lin in Peking was overthrown by Wu Pei-fu, but the superiority of Chang Tso-lin was still maintained in Mukden, which showed that the Japanese imperialists utilized him as a means of retaining control of Manchuria and Mongolia. After the victory of Wu Pei-fu, the Peking government drifted gradually into the hands of pro-American bureaucrats, which was an opportunity for the United States to pursue their Chinese policy. But Wu Pei-fu was not expected—a comparatively progressive militarist—to organize a union government, because if the plans of Wu Pei-fu came into effect the armament would be reduced, the Tu-chün system would be abolished, which would be advantageous for the Chinese bourgeoisie. The American imperialists turned toward an alliance with Japan planning to utilize Chang Tso-lin, Chao Chuen [Ts'ao K'un], and the other conservative militarists and bureaucrats (such as the members of the An-Fu Club, Communicationists Club, etc.) to prevent disagreement between Japan and America, and to form a puppet Chinese government. Great Britain unscrupulously assisted the reactionist General Ch'en Chiung-ming to overthrow Dr. Sun Yat-sen's Nationalist power in Canton. As a matter of fact, it is evident that they used the militarists for their purposes, interrupted the development of the power of the Chinese bourgeoisie and allowed a normal union government under the militarist's power to become the tool of Britain, America and Japan. We may wish to take it for granted that China could establish a so-called union government, but in reality China would never unite, and civil war would never cease until the Great Powers are excluded and the force of the militarists destroyed.

It has been eleven years since the establishment of a Chinese Republic, during which time nearly every year we find civil wars due to the oppression of the nationalists by the militarists or a split among the militarists, of which the Chihli-Anhwei war and the Chihli-Fengtien war are the best examples. At present, the civil wars degenerate into a great confusion, because of the bitter quarrels among the militarists, and the continued unsettled condition of the foreign imperialists. We can never establish the real nationalistic government and secure real peace until the overthrow of the oppression of the militarists and international imperialism. China is still in the period of occupation by militarists. Under the slogan "Unite", there arise two controversial features: one is that the militarists occupy various provinces under the name of "autonomy", and the other is that the North oppresses the South and favors a Mongolian autonomy for the purpose of increasing the militarists' power. Though these two features are different, there is but one idea back of them—to lengthen the militaristic regime. In China proper, including Manchuria, there is no fundamental difference in economic conditions or in nationality. It is irrational to advocate, as have the militarists during ten years, changing the provinces into states, giving as a good reason the necessity for "decentralization" or "autonomy of united provinces" to cover up their selfish purposes. During the last ten years political power has been completely in the hands of the selfish militarists; if decentralization is what we need it will be necessary to make the provinces nations, and the Tuchüns kings. We believe that the principle of federation has been irrationally adopted in China proper. But there are differences between life in China and in Mongolia, Tibet, and Turkestan, which are not only the dwelling places occupied by certain races for long periods of time, but are fundamentally different in economic aspects from China proper. China proper has developed from the stage of petty agricultural handicrafts to the first period of the capitalistic productive system, while Mongolia, Tibet and Turkestan remain in the pastoral stage. If these different races with their different economic phases be compulsorily united under the military control of those who even cannot unite China as it now exists, the result is only to expand the domain of this military control and interrupt the progress of these people towards self-determination and autonomy, with little profit to China proper. In conclusion, the Chinese people should object to the occupation, the so-called autonomy, and the military union, should overthrow all the militarists, and establish the real republic by the union of people themselves; and at the same time according to economic principles they should prevent the expansion of militaristic powers, and respecting the self-determination of the people of Mongolia, Tibet, and Turkestan, they should organize three autonomous nations, and finally reunite these as the China Federal Republic, which will then be the real union of nationalism.

(2)

Originally the foreign imperialists intended to destroy the old Chinese economic structure completely and substitute for it their new capitalistic building, but they do not have the skill necessary to such destruction. They have in many ways interrupted the Chinese economic reform, and they refused to allow the Chinese to build the Canton-Hankow Railway, the Nanking-Hangchow Railway, and the Szechwan-Hankow Railways, and compelled the Manchurian government to loan funds for constructing these railroads, and robbed China of the Han-Yeh-Ping Iron and Coal Mines. These savage actions evoked many furious objections which struck a blow to their monopolistic economic policy. Furthermore, the foreign capitalists who first arrived in China could not act independently, had to ask the Chinese merchants' help and to employ the Chinese as their compradors, brokers and bursars to assist in the exploitation of China. Because of this opportunity to learn occidental business methods the Chinese bourgeoisie gradually completed a first course in industrialism, and during the Great War, when the

European and American commodities were imported into China in less and less volume, while Japanese goods were boycotted, the Chinese bourgeoisie seized the opportunity for development. Since that time Chinese capitalism has step by step prospered along the Yangtze River.

Oppressed by the great organization of capitalism, how can the newly prospering Chinese bourgeoisie freely develop and compete and reach an independent position? They can only become the medium of world capitalism. Moreover, the foreign capitalists for the sake of their own development and to secure special privileges assist the militarists purposely to interrupt the development of young Chinese capitalism so the young Chinese bourgeoisie in order to prevent the economic oppression ought to rise up and struggle against international capitalistic imperialism.

The anti-Japanese movement of 1919 showed that the young Chinese bourgeoisie were able to unite their strength to resist foreign imperialism and the corrupt Peking government. The Canton government, constituted by the Nationalists, was the medium of the Chinese enlightened bourgeoisie. Though the Canton government is now overthrown, the petty bourgeois national movement will never disappear in China. There is a more obvious fact: nationalism will never succeed, unless the intellectual, commercial and industrial class cleverly escape from the plots and plans of deceitful America.

Three hundred million Chinese peasants are the most important factors of our revolutionary movement. The peasants are in misery for several causes,—lack of land, density of population, prevalence of calamity, civil wars and banditry, taxed by the militarists, under pressure from foreign commodities and the increasing cost of living. The peasants may be subdivided into three classes: (1) the rich farmers and landlords; (2) peasants who till their own land; (3) tenants and journeymen. Very few are in the first class, the miserable peasants of the second and third classes are at least ninety-five in percentage. If these poor peasants hope to escape from their miserable environment, there is only one way for them—that is revolution. And it is to be believed that the Chinese revolution will quickly succeed when the majority of the peasants ally with the workers.

Since the foreign commodities choke the Chinese market, the handicraftsmen, small shop-bosses, petty employers are in misery, either bankrupt or losing their occupations. While the home capitalism develops, the misery increases for the handicraftsmen. This great mass suffering from world capitalism of course should join the revolutionary army.

The Chinese labor movement is developing. The strikes of seamen in Hongkong and of other workers for their economic demands, have proved the great power of the workers. The workers' organizations are growing with great speed. The revolutionary movement will certainly develop uninterruptedly as long as the workers are under such extreme oppression from Chinese and foreign capitalists, the result will be a revolutionary army to overthrow world capitalistic imperialism in China.

(3)

Every fact and event proves that what gives the Chinese people (whether he is bourgeois, worker or peasant) the greatest misery is the force of capitalistic imperialism, and of militaristic and bureaucratic feudalism. The revolutionary movement of nationalism to oppose the imperialism and feudalism is very wise. Comparative liberty may be secured, when the national revolution succeeds. We, the proletariat, observe the existing Chinese political and economic conditions, advocate that we, the proletariat and the poor peasants, should assist the national revolutionary movement. We believe that during the struggle, there is only one way to make the real nationalistic revolution come about speedily—that is the cooperation of the proletarian revolutionary forces and the national revolutionary forces.

4.[1] The Duty of the Communist Party of China and the Present Struggle.

It does not mean that the proletariat surrender to the bourgeoisie, when they assist the national revolution. It is the necessary step for the proletariat to take in order to foster their real strength and to shorten the life of feudalism.

We, the proletariat, have our own privileges; when the national revolution succeeds, the proletariat will only secure a little freedom and some rights, and are still not completely emancipated. As soon as nationalism triumphs, the young bourgeoisie will speedily develop standing in the challenging position to oppose the proletarian class. The proletariat should then resist the bourgeoisie, struggling to unite the poor peasants under the Proletarian Dictatorship. If the organization and fighting power are strong, the next step would succeed very soon after the victory of nationalism.

(2)

The Chinese Communist Party is the proletarian political party in China. Our objects are to organize the proletarian class, to establish the soviet dictatorship, to overthrow the private property system, and gradually attain a communistic community through class struggle.

But the Chinese Communist Party, in order to gain immediate advantages to workers and peasants is obliged to direct the workers to assist the national revolutionary movement, and to lead the workers, peasants and petty bourgeoisie to stand on the joint battle line with the Nationalists. For the workers and the poor peasants the goal of the Communist Party of China on the joint battle line are:—
1. To eliminate civil wars, overthrow the militarist party, and lay the foundations for national peace.
2. To overthrow international imperialism in order to reach the complete independence of the Chinese nation.
3. To unite China proper (including Manchuria) as the real Republic of China.
4. To recognize Mongolia, Tibet, and Turkestan as autonomous states.

---
[1] Error. It should be 3.

5. With a free federation, to reunite China Proper, Mongolia, Tibet and Turkestan, and to establish them as the United States of China, a Republic.
6. To demand the unrestricted suffrage of the workers and peasants without discrimination as to sex in the national, provincial, district, municipal and various assemblies, with absolute freedom of speech, press, meeting, assemblage and strike.
7. To enact laws profitable to the workers, peasants, and women:
    A. To better the treatment of workers, by
        a. Abolishing the foreman system.
        b. Inaugurating the eight hour day.
        c. Establishing workers' hospitals and sanitary equipment in the factories.
        d. Providing for factory insurance.
        e. Protecting women workers and child labor.
        f. Reducing unemployment.
    B. To abolish the burdensome poll tax and tax on water transportation, and to provide for the taxation of land in the whole nation—cities and villages.
    C. To abolish the Likin tax and the extra-tax, and to enforce the progressive income tax.
    D. To enact laws for restricting the land rent.
    E. To abolish the laws which restrict the women's rights, and to see that women enjoy equal political, economic and educational rights.
    F. To reform the educational system, to provide for the universal education.

These demands are profitable to all the workers, peasants and petty bourgeoisie, and are necessary to emancipate these classes from the existing oppression. We should unite to struggle for our emancipation! Workers and peasants, come to surround the banner of The Chinese Communist Party.

But the workers should take care not to be the tool of the petty bourgeoisie in the nationalists' joint battle field, and at the same time they must be bold to struggle for our own class privileges. It is most important for the workers to organize in the Communist Party and in the industrial unions. All workers should always remember that they are the independent class, should discipline themselves to prepare for organization and fighting, should prepare the peasants to unite and organize the soviet in order to reach complete emancipation.

The Communist Party of China is a branch of the International Communist Party and it cries out to the Chinese workers and peasants—come together under the banner of the Communist Party to fight! It cries out to the whole oppressed peoples—come, join the workers and peasants under the banner of the Communist Party to struggle together! And it cries to the very mountain tops—come, forward with the world revolution comrades! Union of the proletariat and oppressed nations of the whole world is the only way

of emancipating the whole world!
Forward! All forward!
 Down with the militarists!
  Down with international imperialism!
   Fight for peace!
    Fight for freedom!
     Fight for independence!
      Long live peace, freedom, independence!
       Long live the emancipation of the oppressed masses!
        Long live the Communist Party of China!
         Long live the International Communist Party!

Appendix 4

The Decisions of the Second Conference of the Communist Party of China 1922

(1) **The Decisions concerning the world conditions and the Chinese Communist Party.**

Since the Great War of 1914, the strength of world capitalism has been receding, but on the contrary, the power of the social revolution has come roaring in to high tide. The reason for a temporary ebb in the revolutionary waves is that in the proletarian camps there are many traitors who shamelessly surrender to the bourgeoisie and become the bitterest enemies of the revolutionary proletariat. A condition then arises in which the world imperialists intend to restore their economic supremacy and attack the proletariat throughout the whole world—the most significant indication of the plan is that the capitalists of the various nations are reducing the workers' wages and are increasing their hours of labor. In opposition to this movement the Third International assembles all the proletariat in the world to fight in a joint battle line and to resist the attack of the capitalists.

The Russian Soviet is the first nation of workers and peasants in the world; it is the mother land of the proletariat and the laboring masses; and it is also the camp of the world workers and peasants challenging the world's imperialistic nations. At present the power of world capitalism is still strong, and continuously attacks Russia, so that the labor classes and masses should endeavor to protect her with all their might.

The Chinese Communist Party in its second conference decided to assemble the Chinese workers to enter upon the battle field with the world workers, who protect the proletariat motherland—Soviet Russia, and resist the capitalistic attack; and the party decided to call the oppressed masses of China to help protect Soviet Russia, for Soviet Russia in the forerunner in the emancipation of all oppressed nations.

(2) **The Decision concerning International Imperialism and the Chinese Communist Party.**
1. The important economic conditions of the world at present are:
    A. The economic order of the world has been destroyed by the imperialistic war of 1914-1918.
    B. The capitalistic class is attacking the proletarian class; they are doubling their forces in order to exploit the laboring class and restore the economic order overturned by themselves during the war. The proletariat must unite to resist this attack in a joint battle line.
    C. The capitalist class is planning to seize the raw materials and exploit the laboring classes of the colonies and semi-colonies to make up their losses through the Great War. New conflicts arise within these exploited markets, such as the conflicts between Japan and America, and Great Britain and France, which foment the next imperialistic war.
2. China has enormous natural products and the cheap labor of four hundred million people which makes her the battle field of the world capitalists. This market is now more than ever seriously attracting attention.
3. Chinese capitalism has developed to an extent in which the bourgeoisie are enabled to enlist the feudal militarists on their side to secure special privileges. The foreign imperialists, hoping to secure greater special privileges, assist the Chinese feudal militarists in order that the Chinese bourgeoisie may be kept down.
4. Under this condition, the power of the revolution of 1911 has become very weak; China, during the last eleven years, is still burdened and oppressed under the militarists' civil wars and acts of violence, which cause interruption of the bourgeois industry and commerce; the peasants are unbearably tortured, and the miseries of the workers increase.
5. China Proper is occupied by feudal militarists. General Wu Pei-fu intrigues to unite the North and South by military force, and now reassembles the Old Parliament as an evidence of his good intentions, all in vain.
6. China cannot unite her territories because the economic condition of these domains is entirely different from that of China Proper; other differences also exist among Chinese territories.
7. The realization of the dream for a unified China will come when she escapes from world imperialism, when she overthrows the feudal militarists, and when she establishes the really unified nation.
8. The Second Conference of the Chinese Communist Party decided that the main efforts of the party should be as follows:

a. To put down the civil war, overthrow the militarists and establish national peace.
   b. To unify China Proper (including Manchuria) into a real Democratic Republic.
   c. To overthrow the oppression of international imperialism and to achieve the absolute independence of the Chinese nation.
   d. To recognize the autonomy of Mongolia, Tibet, and Turkestan.
   e. To reunite Mongolia, Tibet and Turkestan into a United Republic of China based upon the principle of federation.
   f. To secure various liberties.
   g. To enact laws protecting workers, peasants, women and children.
9. If these foregoing objects should be achieved all the workers, peasants and petty bourgeoisie under the existing order would be helped, and these classes should join the fight for those rights.
10. In order to accomplish these ends the Chinese workers should unite under the C.C.C.[1] banner, on the one hand participating in the national revolutionary battle line, and on the other hand struggling to improve their own conditions.
11. It is necessary for the Chinese workers to unite in various organizations as component parts of the Chinese Communist Party.
12. To aid the working class is the prime object of the Chinese Communist Party. We join the nationalists' battle line so that the working class may secure political power at the outset, and therefore the construction of a Nationalist joint battle line is one of our policies.

(3) The Decision concerning the Nationalist Joint Battle Line.

The economic and political evolution of human beings constitutes the class struggle. During the period between feudalism and democracy, because of the economic and political changes, it is inevitable for the bourgeoisie to fight against feudalism. In like manner during the period of the change from democracy to communism, it is also inevitable for the proletariat to challenge the bourgeoisie in the changes economic and political.

The history of humanity is a record of struggle. The great war waged by the proletariat against the bourgeoisie is still not at an end, and that of democracy against feudalism is still raging. Especially in Oriental nations, young in their industries, the power of feudalism still exists in social traditions as well as in national sovereignty. Within those nations the lives and property of the people are firmly grasped in military hands, and the force of laws and public opinion upholds this state of affairs. For the common welfare, it is necessary for democracy to overthrow feudalism. If the proletariat cannot bring on revolution alone, they must be assisted to fight feudalism.

---

[1] Probably should be either C.P.C. or C.C.P.

The feudal militarist party is the joint enemy of proletariat and nationalist. No freedom of the press, meeting, or assembly, is obtainable unless these two classes unite, and no class can gain an opportunity to develop if they cannot secure these liberties. After the Nationalists achieve success they in turn desiring certain privileges will naturally oppress the proletariat by means of the political powers they have seized from feudal rulers. When that time comes the power of the proletariat over the bourgeoisie will depend upon the ability to organize and fight which they will have shown during the period of the revolution.

China is republic in name, but is really controlled by the feudal militarists in fact. Externally it is a semi-independent nation controlled by international imperialistic powers. Under such economic and political conditions, and under such internal and external double pressure, the proletariat, because there is no other way to secure freedom, must fight for it, that is, join the national revolutionary movement. We ought to realize that this joining does not mean that we surrender to the nationalists who only represent the bourgeoisie, to be their vassals, and also by no means does it follow that the victory of the nationalists will be the complete emancipation of the proletariat; but it is a fact that temporary union with the nationalists is necessary for us to overthrow the pressure of our enemies—the feudal militarists internally and the international imperialists externally, otherwise the proletariat ought to join and assist the nationalists, but by no means to give up the management of their own party because the Nationalist party is not the party that represents the proletariat and does not struggle for the proletariat. On the contrary, they should assemble the proletarian party—under the banner of C.C.P.—and strive for their own class independently.

The communists are not the utopians or the revolutionary candidates, but are the party which at any time stand for indefatigable work. Under the economic and political conditions of China and the Chinese proletariat, we recognize that a national revolution will profit not only the bourgeoisie but also the proletariat. As a matter of fact we should unite all the revolutionary parties, organize a joint battle line with the nationalists in order to realize our object of overthrowing the feudal militarist party and imperialistic oppression, and to establish a real democratic independent nation. We should summon all the workers and peasants to join the struggle under our banner. We should tell them this struggle, though it will not completely release them from their miseries, is the first step toward aiding the workers and peasants and leads to the road where their right may be established. We should again tell them this joint struggle is not for the Nationalists' profit; we are not sacrificing ourselves for the Nationalists but fight only to gain temporary freedom. The proletariat must not forget their own independent organization during the struggle.

The Second Conference of the C.C.P. approves the policy of joining the Nationalist joint battle line as proposed by the Central Executive Committee because it meets the urgent needs of present conditions. It should subsquently be expanded as follows

A. The Nationalist Party and the Young Socialist Group are called upon to open a representative conference in a suitable place to discuss the best method of summoning other revolutionary parties and working out a program.
B. The members of parliament favoring communism are asked to unite and form a left wing of the Democratic Alliance.
C. The labor unions, peasant groups, merchants associations, teachers associations, students associations, womens political alliances, lawyers clubs, and editors clubs of various cities are summoned to organize the "Democratic Alliance".

(4) The Decision concerning the Chinese Communist Party to join the Third International.

The proletarian class is cosmopolitan, and the proletarian revolution is also cosmopolitan. The revolutionary influence must by no means be allowed to increase except to unite the world proletariat, especially in the young Oriental industrial nations. The only existing proletarian revolutionary camp which represents the world proletarian class is the Third International, newly formed after the Russian revolution. The Third International opposes the Second International, which uses the proletarian on one side and is the puppet of capitalistic imperialism on the other. As the Chinese Communist Party is the party representing the Chinese proletariat, the second conference formally decided to become members of the "Third International", completely to recognize the twenty-one articles decided upon by the Third International, and to be a branch party of the Third International.

(5) The Decision concerning the Parliamentary Action.
1. In the nations whose economic condition may be described as advanced, the large scale capitalistic production has been developed for many years, and the parliamentary politics which parallels this capitalism together make an almost invincible stronghold. Under such an influence the communists who became part of the governing class tend to drop their revolutionary ideas and begin to plan to reform conditions through parliamentary action. This has been the case among German, Austrian, French, and Belgian social democrats.
2. After the Second International had surrendered to capitalistic ideas because of the stress of war conditions, the Third International was born. It decided that action through existing legal bodies had some value (contrary to the theory upheld by the Second International), and determined that its members should seek places in existing governing bodies in order to correct the false doctrines set forth by the Second International.
3. China, backward in the economic struggle becomes partly the exploited field and semi-colony of the international capitalistic imperialists, and also partly the prey of the militarist force organized by the international capitalistic imperialism. The previous revolution, although national

in scope, was not successful; parliamentary politics were not firmly established. Though various assemblages are summoned, they are always menaced by pressure, interfered with and tortured by the military force.
4. The Chinese Communist Party is the hope of the Chinese proletariat and poor peasant masses. It should rush into parliament which is menaced by the feudal militarist party and the communist party there should [fight?] against the political evils originating in the military power and continued with the aid of the imperialists. In Parliament it should not neglect to preach the idea of revolution and in the various assemblies should fight for all benefits than can be secured for the proletariat and poor peasant class.
5. The Chinese Communist Party, in order to arouse the revolutionary parliamentary action, recognizes the principles passed by the Second Conference of the Third International. (The principles passed by the Third International may have perhaps been published in the American newspapers and are here omitted.) [1]

(6) The Decision concerning the Labor Union Movement and the Chinese Communist Party.

The labor movement of China can hardly shake off the bondage of old guilds and handicraft unions. The struggle of the labor class is only a sporadic movement under the particular conditions of a certain handicraft or in a certain factory. These movements are not nation-wide. The labor organization is not strong, and the members of the unions are not very great in number. As these defects are realized it becomes the duty of the Chinese Communist Party to concentrate on enlarging and properly directing the labor movement.

Considering the present condition of the Chinese labor movement, our past activities and experience, and the results of discipline in modern European labor movements, the following are adopted as our fundamental policies:—

1. When the working classes and labor masses struggle to release themselves from the exploitation of bourgeoisie, it is necessary for them to join the most advanced of the struggling elements—the proletariat of the labor masses. The Chinese Communist Party should concentrate its efforts upon influencing such possible members of the labor union as railway workers, seamen, metal workers, textile workers, etc.
2. Why should a labor union be formed? It is the means of protecting the laborers' profits and struggle for such profits. Workers produce goods, therefore they should enjoy the things they produce. This is the very starting point of the labor union.
3. A labor union should make clear and recognize that there can be no similarity of interest between capitalists and workers. No conflict be-

---
[1] Clearly an insertion by Ch'en.

tween these two camps with regard to profits can be harmonized. It is not only unnecessary for labor unions to try to harmonize the differences between capitalists and workers, but it is necessary for them to make this antagonism more bitter. One struggle in which the workers are victorious will help them to fight again. The labor organization will become stronger with each victory. It is necessary for the workers to invest the greater part of their funds for strikes, yet at the same time, the workers must be careful to choose an opportune moment for calling a strike.

4. The labor unions should endeavor to improve the condition of the workers. The labor union should plan speedily to achieve the end and aim of the labor movement, e.g., the overthrow wage-slavery and to reconstruct society according to communistic principles.

5. When the labor union organizes to improve the conditions of labor, it should join the movement to further labor legislation. We should warn the labor unions that they must be strong before demanding labor legislation and the improvement of the conditions of labor. Under the capitalistic system, labor legislation and improved labor conditions can only be achieved when the union is strong enough to threaten the government and employers and thereby enforce its will.

6. Some of our comrades often hold that the labor unions should not become a political movement. This is the tendency of anarchical syndicalism, which is a great mistake. It usually causes labor unions to become weak, and makes them occupy an illegal position. Labor unions should struggle politically for the national independence, citizens' right and liberties (including universal suffrage and the legality of the strikes in the penal law), and should occupy an independent and important position in the Nationalist joint battle line, and then the workers can speedily secure an ultimate triumph. It has been said that joining the Nationalist revolutionary forces is only an opportune measure, and not in accord with communist precepts. This is not true. It is important for the proletariat to lead themselves; no non-proletarian workers are allowed to be leaders.

7. When a labor union decided [decides?] to oppose an individual, such as a foreman in a factory, or a whole class of individuals, such as the owners of said factory, they must conduct such opposition according to general communistic ideas, and not as a private disagreement.

8. There are two most important things in the labor union which must be sought after. One is "collective bargaining" and the other is the "equal wages for equal work". Individual contract is profitable for employers and helps them to exploit the worker. By this means they can employ or discharge workers arbitrarily and control the wages of labor. The union must hold that no contract or employment or agreement on conditions of work can be made individually. All such contracts must be made by the representatives of the employees and em-

ployers. Classification of wages according to race, sex, age, and strength is the most cunning and cruel means of the capitalists to deceive the laboring class. By these means the capitalists not only more selfishly exploit the weak and young workers, but break up the labor class into numerous factions differently paid, in order to make them jealous of each other and willing to compete with their fellow-workers. In such cases, the labor union should strongly advocate "equal wages for equal work". No matter whether a worker is foreigner or Chinese, man or woman, adult, child or aged, equal wages must be paid if they can perform the same work; no different scale of wages is allowed on the ground of biological or social differences. Equal wages does not mean to reduce the higher wages to equalize the lower, but to raise the lower to equal the higher. Insistence upon these two principles are the fundamental duties of the labor unions.

9. The nature of the labor union is very different from that of the guilds. No employers are allowed to become members, and on the other hand, all wage-earners are expected to become members. No sex, age, religion, race, nationality, political opinions, skill or lack of skill is discriminated against. Labor unions are not permitted to contribute extra-fees or to restrict the membership through investigations which are too petty. To make the union a union for the masses is the first thing for us to remember.
10. The principal activity of labor unions is to struggle with the capitalist and with the government; mutual aid and mutual understanding are the next important objects, for the union is a fighting union, and not only an organ to secure benefits.
11. The labor union must have a good school within itself. It should spend most of its time in educating its members. The practical effects of a labor union must be taught as an important course in order that the class consciousness of workers may be developed.
12. The structure of each labor union must be speedily made into a firmly united, centralized, disciplined industrial unit. Within such union no autonomous groups are allowed to be formed according to occupations, for this would weaken the union to struggle.
13. In the labor unions, the first tenet of organization is the factory committee. The workers of a factory in a special industry should organize a factory committee as a fundamental unit, upon which the industrial union is organized. But the committee should be an organization of wage earners only—workers; no complication due to membership of employers and labor representatives is allowed. And the committee is not allowed to be independent of the industrial union.
14. The labor union founded only on the industrial union is still not regarded as the best form of union. The best form of union is the one based on industry but looking forward to changing conditions by revolution. Such a union puts itself under general communistic disci-

pline. To unite the whole labor class, there must be no friction between workers in any particular union, and no conflict between unions throughout the whole nation.
15. In every country there is coordination of the revolutionary labor unions concerning the struggle with world capitalism. The united associations of world revolutionary labor unions is the Red International Labor League. The Chinese Communist Party founded upon the above-mentioned principles should organize labor unions and lead under the banner of the International Labor Unions. The Chinese Communist Party should not let the Chinese laboring class suffer from an influx of foreign labor but should raise the wages of Chinese labor in order to prevent exploitation by foreign capitalists.
16. The difference between the communist party and the labor union is this: the Communist Party is the army of all the class-conscious elements, is the herald of the proletariat, has a definite platform, and is the proletarian party, whose object is to overthrow the bourgeoisie and capitalism; the labor union is the union of all workers (no matter what their political opinions are); it tries to educate socialistic and communistic spirits, to push forward the same objects of communism, but advances comparatively slowly. As in war, every military body must have a leader, behind whom the great mass of the army advances, the Communist Party may be regarded as a leader, the workers as the army. The Communist Party, which in any labor movement is the head, must pay attention to the labor union's activity, and lead the labor union movement honestly and boldly.
17. The Communist Party is the practical head of the labor unions and is the spokesman of the proletarian class. It should organize strong groups in the labor unions, factory committees and other laboring groups, omitting none.
18. The Communist, when active in the labor unions organized by the Nationalist, Anarchistic or Christian parties, is not permitted to direct other workers to leave these organized unions. The Communist tactics are to increase their own influence in those labor unions to such an extent that they can overthrow the leadership of the Nationalist, anarchistic or Christian parties and assume control themselves.
19. In the struggle to increase the well-being of the workers, we, the communists, should prepare to cooperate with the nationalists, the anarchists, and even the Christians at any time. But we should at the same time make them understand that only the Communist Party is the true workers' and laborers' political party.

The Additional Decision:

The above-mentioned decisions are the most important decisions concerning the labor union movement for workers in important industries. There are a few less important points as shown in the following:

1. The cooperative associations formed by the labor party should be self-supporting and should help only the laboring class and should be managed by the Communist Party.
2. The Communist Party is asked to be active in the progressive guilds. The reason is that the employers may be excluded later, and the new guilds of the same nature or engaged in the same sort of production be united to organize labor unions.
3. The Communist Party should also be active in the conservative guilds and the groups organized by the bourgeoisie for deceiving the workers, within which small communist groups ought to be organized.

(7) The Decision concerning Young Men Movement Problem.

(1)

With the process of machine productivity, the young and weak have become victimized to supply labor for the exploiting system. In many an enterprise the young labor army has entered and they have become as important an appendage of the machines as the adult workers. The treatment with regard to conditions of work and pay of the young laborers by capitalists is generally more cruel than that toward adults. The young workers have become the more exploited class.

Not only were the young men of the proletariat oppressed by the bourgeoisie, but when conflict arose they were pressed into service to defend their very oppressors. In every nation which has developed through capitalism and imperialism a strong armament is necessary. Many millions of strong young workers are used to maintain defensive and offensive forces. The imperialistic nations not only use their armament to exploit weak nations, but to put down the resistance and revolution of their own laboring class. In every war and rebellion the workers are organized into an army driven by the bourgeoisie and are often made to destroy their own homes and foreign brothers. In order to maintain the bourgeois supremacy in trade competition no one knows how many billions of young men in the very flower of youth have shed blood during the history of capitalism.

Under this cruel exploitation and shameful utilization by the bourgeoisie, the pioneers of European young labor uplift their resisting flag. They struggle boldly for their economic benefits, and oppose militarism. Unfortunately for the movement, many young workers have been played upon and influenced by the yellow socialists, so that they did not carry out their revolutionary aims to the end. The Berlin Conference of November 1919 was the assemblage of international proletarian young men who hated the slaughter of imperialistic war. This conference has been successful in organizing the Red International Association of Proletarian Young Men—the Young Communist International. The second conference of the Young Communist International adopted the slogan, "Go among the laboring mass," determined what was the new duty of struggling young laborers, decided to lead the proletarian young labor movement independently under the political leadership of the International Communist Party.

Any place where the young men are exploited is the place for the young communists to be active. They should organize and direct their fellows for various economic struggles. This will prove an effectual way to attract them to the communistic revolutionary army's banner.

The ability to push the capitalistic world into its own grave already yawning depends upon the increase of knowledge among the laboring class. The most important thing in the young proletarian movement is the revolutionary education, material for which can be easily sought out in their daily struggle. The organization itself should be the disciplined instructor; every movement should be a course in disciplining the young workers into the class conscious revolutionary elements.

Help the Red Army of the world workers' motherland—Soviet Russia—oppose the armament of the bourgeoisie.

The economic order of the world has been destroyed by imperialism. The bourgeoisie are now exploiting their own workers and the weak nations in order to restore the economic conditions previous to 1914. In opposing these measures the young workers would be the first to fall. The necessity of the present time is that the young workers unite [with?] the adults on the international joint battle line to resist this attack.

(2)

China, with its numerous products and 400,000,000 cheap labor people has been the object of exploitation and competition by the British, French, Japanese and American imperialists during the last eighty years. The economic life of China is clutched in the foreign capitalists' hands, and politics are controlled by the reactionary feudal militarists who, controlled by foreign imperialists, are selfish for their own ends, [and] occupy various provinces in order to wage war against each other.

Capitalism in China [although it?] has developed to the degree that the newly arising bourgeoisie could rise up and resist the foreign powers, overthrow feudalism and establish an independent union, has not succeeded since 1912, because it has been under the oppression of imperialism and feudalism.

This condition determines the duty of the young communists' struggle in China. The young men movement should not only struggle for the economic and cultural advancement of the young workers, should not only organize them into a proletarian revolutionary army under the dictatorship of communism and the Young Men's International, but should gather in all the young men's revolutionary forces for the nationalist joint battle line, and lead them to struggle—to overthrow the imperialistic and feudalistic forces.

The Communist Party should remember that the welfare of young workers is the first object. It should recognize that the struggle for a national revolution is the only chance to organize a proletarian revolution. It should absorb the strength and solidarity of the revolutionary young labor mass.

(3)

The second conference of the Chinese Communist Party recognizes that the platform and decisions of the Young Socialist Group in its first national conference are the foundations upon which to base all practical revolutionary plans. It also recognizes the importance of the Chinese Communist movement.

Concerning the relation between the Young Socialist Group of China and the Chinese Communist Party, the Young Socialist Group is the independent party on the side of young workers with regard to bettering their economic conditions, but for purposes of a general political movement, the Young Socialist Group should always be controlled by the Chinese Communist Party.

In order to maintain the close relationship of these two parties, and to ensure the co-operation of the various movements, the Conference recognizes the necessity of sending representatives from the various grades in each organization to confer with each other. How this should be done should be decided upon and carried out by the Central Executive Committees of those two parties.

(8) The Decision concerning the Women Movement.

(1)

For several centuries, the principles of equality as well as of liberty have been emblazoned on the banner of capitalistic civilization. Under this system where economic conditions are actually not equal, women cannot secure any equality or liberty. They not only become the cheaper productive slaves of the capitalists in the labor markets, but must bear the burden of homekeeping and motherhood under the capitalistic social organization. Under such a system emancipation for women can never be obtained.

The only place where women begin to realize equality and liberty is Soviet Russia. They have secured equal rights in politics, economics and society. They have undertaken the practical work of social reconstruction, without aid from men. The community maternity hospitals, community restaurants, community baths and asylums for children are in process of establishment. All this proves that the equality and freedom women get under the dictatorship of proletariat within five years is far more than what the women receive under the dictatorship of the bourgeoisie in a century. It is also proved that the complete emancipation of women will be realized only after the success of socialism.

(2)

Since the entry of international exploitation in China, the proletarian women have been degraded to the position of wage slaves. They work over twelve hours a day under almost unbearable conditions, and receive only half as much wages as the men workers are paid. The treatment of women and children in the labor group is extremely inhumane.

Under the existing order, the proletarian women are already tortured in the cruel way, there are still many who formerly did not belong to the laboring class who are driven to the army of factory labor, and many more women in China imprisoned in the bondage of feudal rites who live prostitute-like lives. As to the economic, political and educational rights, it is without doubt the common condition of all classes of women in the whole country to be deprived thereof. The Chinese Communist Party besides endeavoring to struggle for equal wages, proper labor legislation for women and child labor laws, should also struggle to emancipate all oppressed women in China, without consideration as to class.

The Chinese Communist Party believes that the emancipation of women is helped by emancipation of the laboring class in general. They can release themselves when the proletariat secure the political power. The demands of the Chinese Communist Party at present for women are: (1) to help women to secure the rights of universal suffrage and political rights and liberty, (2) to protect the women and children in industry, (3) to put down all the bondage of all old social rites and traditions. The Chinese Communist Party cries loudly to all women: Our movement is only the necessary step to reach the goal of emancipation. Under the private property system it is impossible for women really to emancipate themselves. Forward, the road to freedom is just ahead.

(3)

The Third International is the world revolution headquarters of all proletarian classes, all oppressed nations, all oppressed women and all oppressed young men, of which the Communist Women's International is a department. In the third conference, the Third International decided that in every nation a special committee should be organized in the communist party to lead the women, a women's department should be elected and a special column should be opened for women in the communist newspapers. The Chinese Communist Party decided to adopt this plan as soon as it can.

(9) The Decision concerning the Constitution of the Chinese Communist Party.

We, the Communist Party, are neither the Marxian institution organized by the intellectuals nor a fanatic revolutionary group with few Communists unrelated to the masses. We should be the true political party organized by the proletarian mass, full of the revolutionary spirit, willing to struggle for the proletariat and should be the leader of the proletarian revolutionary movement. As we are neither lecturing intellectuals nor fanatic revolutionists, we need not go to universities, research clubs and libraries. As we are the fighting political party of the proletariat, we only need to go among the masses, to organize a "mass party". As we want to organize a revolutionary and a great mass party, we should remember two important laws: (1) All action of the Communist Party should be related to the great mass of laborers. The communists should go among every class of working men and teach their doctrine. (2) The one aim of those at the controlling center of the party should be to prepare and discipline their members so that they will be ready for a revolution when the time is ripe.

In any revolutionary party, if serious, centralized and trained organization and discipline is lacking, then it only has the desire for revolution, and has insufficient strength to struggle to work out the revolutionary movement.

The serious, centralized, disciplined organization is formed according to the following principles:

1. To avoid a riotous condition, the organization from the Central down to the small group should have a serious object. To avoid symptoms of anarchy, it should have centralized and iron-like laws.
2. Every comrade should be trained by the party to almost military discipline in his actions.
3. Every comrade should not only express his communistic ideals in his speech, but it is important for him to show that he is a communist by his actions.
4. Every comrade should sacrifice his own opinions, feelings and advancement to protect the unity of the party.
5. Every comrade should remember that when he is not active for the Communist Party on any day, he is one who destroys communism on that day.
6. No matter in what place or at what time his speech should be the party's speech, his actions such as would be prescribed by the party. He should not possess any individual interest apart from the party. Any activity apart from the party's control is completely his individual activity and not the party's activity; it becomes the anarchical communism.
7. Every comrade should understand that when the party enforces its dictatorship and discipline, it does not do so after the fashion of the bourgeois laws and orders, but enforces its will in preparation of the revolution.

The second national conference decided that the Chinese Communist Party will not succeed as an institution nor as a utopian revolutionary group, but will succeed as a great party sufficiently strong to carry out a proletarian revolution. Our organization should be seriously centralized and drilled. Our action should not separate from those of the mass.

Appendix 5

The Organization of the Communist Party of China

CHAPTER 1
Membership

1. No discrimination as to nationality or sex exists in the membership. Anyone who believes in the principles of our party, who will submit himself to the discipline of the party and who will devotedly serve our party, is allowed to become a member.
2. When an individual wishes to join the party, he should be introduced by one of the party members to the local executive committee who should report to the sectional executive committee who, in turn, should report to the central committee. When the sectional and central committees have investigated and passed upon the candidate he becomes a formal member. When a worker enters the party, only the consent of the sectional committee and report to the central committee by the sectional committee are necessary.
3. Anyone, recognized by the central executive committee as being a communist of any communist party recognized by the Third International, can become a member of our party.

CHAPTER 2
Organization

4. In every village, factory, railway, mine, regiment, or community surrounding such units where there are from three to five communists, a group may be organized in which a leader is elected to act under the jurisdiction of the local branch party. In a place where no local branch party exists, the sectional executive committee may decide upon the arrangement of those groups under the nearest branch party or under the sectional party directly; in a place where there is no sectional executive committee, the groups are supervised and directed by the central executive committee. Where more than two groups exist, a number of members may be appointed by the local executive committee to represent the quarter of the various groups of that organ. The organization in groups is the regular method of organization in our party, and forms a unit of discipline and activity which all members should enter.
5. In any locality, when more than two communist units exist, deputies may be sent by the sectional executive committee, with the consent of the central executive committee, to that locality to summon the members to an assembly or to select representatives for an assembly, which [may?] elect three members to organize the local executive committee. At the same time, three candidates are elected in order to assume con-

trol when the committee leaves. Where there is no sectional executive committee a deputy may be sent by the central executive committee to summon the members to organize the local committee under the direct jurisdiction of the central executive committee. The control of the sectional committee may be taken over by the executive committee.

6. In any section, where there are more than two local executive committees, the central executive committee may send deputies to summon the representatives to elect five members to organize the sectional executive committee and simultaneously to elect three candidates in order to fill vacancies. In case of necessity, the central committee may appoint one of the local committee temporarily to take charge in place of the sectional committee. The jurisdiction of the sectional committee is limited and may be changed by the central committee.

7. Five members are elected by the National Representatives Conference to organize the central executive committee, and three candidates are at the same time elected to fill any vacancy on this committee.

8. The tenure of office of members of the central executive committee is one year, of the sectional and local committees half a year, while length of time the head of a group holds office is uncertain, but all can continue their post through re-election. The officers of the various local groups are appointed and dismissed by the local committee arbitrarily.

9. The central executive committee enforces the decisions of the National Conference, examines and decides the policies and actions of the party; the sectional and local committees enforce the decisions made by the central executive committee, and within their limits and competency examine and decide upon the method of procedure. In each committee, a chairman should be elected to take charge of affairs and accounts; the rest of the members of the committee assist the chairman to take charge of political questions, labor difficulties; of young men and women movements, each committee having one of these matters in charge.

10. The regulations passed by the National Conference or Central executive committee are carried out and the special problems arising in the various places are managed by a special deputy committee consisting of certain members appointed by the sectional and local committees. When the special deputy committee meets, one member of the executive committee should be chairman.

CHAPTER 3
Conference

11. In the various groups, a conference should be called weekly by the head; in small units, all members or heads of the groups should meet once a month; in various localities, the units should be summoned by

the local executive committee monthly; every half year all the members or heads of groups should meet once in each locality; the executive committee should summon the representatives for a conference in that locality once each half year; the national conference of representatives should be summoned for a definite term by the central executive committee once a year.
12. If necessary, the central executive committee may summon the provisional conference of national representatives. When petitioned by the majority of the sections, such a provisional conference of representatives should also be summoned by the central committee.
13. The number of the representatives to the national conference or provisional national conference is provided provisionally by the central executive committee.
14. When a special problem concerning a certain district arises, a higher executive committee may command a lower executive committee to summon the members of that district for a conference.
15. The central committee may at any time send a deputy to various places to summon a special conference, in which the deputy sent by the central committee should be the chairman.
16. In the central, sectional or local executive committee, the conference should be called by the chairman.

CHAPTER 4
Discipline

17. The national conference of representatives is the highest organ of the party, but during the period when the conference is not sitting, the central executive committee becomes the highest organ.
18. The decisions of the national conference and central executive committee should be accepted absolutely by all members.
19. The commands of the higher organs of the party should be enforced by the lower committees. If such enforcement should not be forthcoming, the committees may be dissolved, and reorganized by the central governing bodies of the party.
20. When the majority of the members protest against the commands of the local executive committee, the protest may be carried to the sectional executive committee for judgment. When the local executive committee protests against the command of the sectional executive committee, the central executive committee decides upon the justice of the protest. When there is opposition to the rulings of the central executive committee, such opposition may be carried to the national conference or to a special national conference for a decision. But all such orders should be enforced until revoked by the proper committee.
21. The local or sectional executive committee and various groups should carry out and teach the policies decided upon by the central executive

committee; no policies can be settled upon by the local committee itself. When an important problem relative to the whole nation arises, the local or sectional executive committee is not allowed to express its own opinion alone, before the central executive committee states its opinion. If the opinion held by the local or sectional executive committee is contrary to the decisions and settled policies of the party, reorganization of that committee may be ordered by the central executive committee.
22. Any member of the party, unless by special consent of the central executive committee, is not permitted to enter another political party or group; when entering our party, he who has been a member of any other political party or group should formally resign from that party or group, unless he has the consent of the central executive party to remain in it.
23. The member, unless with the special consent of the central executive committee, is not allowed to be any state official of a capitalistic nation.
24. All the policies of the party are decided upon by majority vote, and such policies must be absolutely obeyed even by the minority who may have voted against them.
25. Any member who is found guilty of the following should be expelled by the local executive committee:
    a. Opposing in speech or action the manifesto and regulation of the party, and the decisions of the national representatives conference or various executive committees.
    b. Continually failing to attend meetings without any good reason.
    c. Failing to pay the party dues for three months.
    d. Failing to serve the party in whatever duty may be assigned for four weeks without reason.
    e. Failing to acknowledge the error of his ways after restoration of membership, following investigation.
    f. Disclosing the secrets of the party.

    When the local executive committee expels a member, the reason therefore should be reported to the central and sectional executive committees.

CHAPTER 5
Revenue

26. The revenues of the party are obtained as follows:
    (1) Monthly contributions. Each member should contribute monthly one dollar, when his or her wages are under fifty dollars; if the wages exceed fifty dollars, ten percent should be contributed; any person without monthly wages, or a worker receiving under twenty dollars a month, should contribute twenty cents; the unemployed or imprisoned member is exempted.

(2) Extra-contribution within the party.
(3) Subsidy outside the party.
27. The revenues and expenditures of the party are controlled by the central executive committee.

CHAPTER 6
Supplementary rule

28. The right to amend the regulations belongs to the National Conference of Representatives; the right to interpret these regulations belongs to the Central Executive Committee.
29. These regulations are passed by the Second National Representatives Conference of the Communist Party of China (16th to 23rd of July, 1922) and are valid from the date announced by the Central Executive Committee.

Appendix 6
The Manifesto of the Third Conference of the Chinese Communist Party 1923

The people of China are oppressed by two forces, the Great Powers externally and the militarists internally, and the life of the nation and the freedom of the people are in extreme danger. This is felt not only by the industrial and agricultural workers and students, but is gradually being perceived by the peaceful and conservative merchants.

The complicated force of the political situation in the Peking government; the really severe oppression of the labor organizations and students' associations under the control of the Peiyang militarists; the wickedness of the soldiers and bandits in Shantung and Hunam [Hunan] provinces; the irrational demands of the Powers even threatening to annul the advantages promised to China in the Washington Conference; the violence of the Japanese sailors in Shashi and Changsha; the forced exportation of cotton demanded by the Powers; the civil wars of the Canton province instigated by the war lords Wu Pei-fu and Ch'i Hsi-yüan; and also the future war expected by the Chihli and Fengtien militarists and the local struggles of the Chihli militarists,—are strong proof that these hardships fall heaviest upon the citizens, who, except through concentrating their own efforts toward the communist form of government can find no other way to emancipate themselves; and those facts are strong proof that the movement for a national revolution which we are furthering by the slogans "Down with militarism" and "Down with international imperialism" is the right road to achieve this end.

The National Party of China should be the central force of the national revolution, and should lead the forces to effect the national revolution; but unfortunately the Nationalists have two ideas, e.g., (1) they hope the Powers will help the Chinese in a national revolution, which is actually asking help from the enemy, [which] not only would cause the Nationalists to lose leadership in the revolution, but would make the people depend upon a foreign power, and would discourage the spirit of independence and self-confidence in the people. (2) They concentrate their efforts only upon military action, without paying any attention to the need for propaganda among the people. For these two reasons, the Nationalists lose their political leadership and we believe that the national revolutionists because of their lack of the sympathy with the people will never succeed with only military action.

We still hope that all of the social revolutionary elements will join the Nationalists in order that a national revolution may come about rapidly; at the same time we also hope that the Nationalists will dare to abandon their two old ideas of dependence upon the Powers, and the concentration of their efforts upon military action. We hope that they will pay more attention to political propaganda among the masses in order to establish the real central forces of the social welfare and real leadership for the national revolution.

Considering the political and economic features of the international situation and particularly China, considering the misery and want of the Chinese social classes (workers, peasants and merchants) a national revolution is necessary. We, the Chinese Communist Party, cannot for a minute neglect the workers and peasants; our special duty is to educate and organize the workers and peasants; to direct the workers and peasants to participate in the national revolution is our most important task. Our first mission is to emancipate the oppressed Chinese nation by means of a national revolution, and next to work for the world revolution, to emancipate the oppressed nations and oppressed classes of the whole world.

All hail to the Chinese national revolution!

Success to the emancipation of the oppressed classes in all nations of the world!

Success to the emancipation of the oppressed nations throughout the world!

BIBLIOGRAPHY

Abbott, J. F.	Japanese Expansion and American Policies.
Baker, R. S.	The Versailles Treaty and After.
	Journal Current History, January, 1924.
Brown, H. J.	The Mastery of the Far East.
China Year Book	1921, 1922, and 1923.
Chia, S. Y.	The Financial History of the Republic of China.
Clements, P. H.	The Boxer Rebellion.
Chu, C.	The Tariff Problem in China.
Dickinson, G. L.	Cause of International War.
Engels, F.	Socialism Utopian and Scientific.
"Forward"	A Chinese Communist Party Magazine.
Hayes, C. J. H.	A Political and Social History of Modern Europe, Vols. 1 & 2.
Hayes, C. J. H.	A Brief History of the Great War.
Hsu, C.	Railway Problem in China.
Hyndman, H. M.	The Evolution of Revolution.
Huang, F. H.	Public Debt in China.
Hughes, C. E.	The Foreign Policy of the United States. Text of address at Philadelphia, November 30, 1923.
Laidler, H. W.	Socialism in Thought and Action.
Li, C. S.	Central and Local Finance in China.
Lenin, N.	Soviet at Work.
Kautsky, K.	The Social Revolution.
Kirkup, T.	A History of Socialism.
Marx and Engels	Communist Manifesto.
Millard, T. F.	Our Eastern Question.
Morse, H. B.	International Relations of the Chinese Empire.
Olgin, M. J.	The Soul of the Russian Revolution.
Overbach [Overlach], T. W.	Foreign Financial Control in China.
Postgate, R. W.	The Workers' International.
Rose [Ross], E. A.	The Russian Bolshevik Revolution.
Rowntree, J.	The Imperial Drug Trade.
Russell, B.	A Proposed Road to Freedom.

Reinsch, P. S. — Colonial Administration.
Sargent, A. J. — Anglo-Chinese Commerce and Diplomacy.
Seligman, D. [E.] R. A. — The Economic Interpretation of History.
Simkhovitch, V. G. — Marxism versus Socialism.
Sun Yat-sen — The International Development of China.
Sun Yat-sen — The Policy of Construction of the Nation. (in Chinese)
Trotsky, L. — The Bolsheviki and World Peace.
Spargo, J. — Arner, G. L., The Elements of Socialism.
Verblen [Veblen], T. — The Theory of Business Enterprise.
Webb and Sidney [Webb, Sidney and Beatrice] — The Decay of Capitalist Civilization.
Willoughby, W. W. — Foreign Rights and Interest in China.
Weyl, W. E. — American World Problem.
Woolf, L. — Economic Imperialism.
Young China — A Chinese Daily Press in San Francisco.
Young, G. — The Machinery of Diplomacy.